Never Mind

Also by
Wayne (Ram Tzu) Liquorman:

NO WAY for the Spiritually "Advanced"

Acceptance of What IS...a book about Nothing

Never Mind

A Journey Into Non-Duality With Wayne Liquorman

Edited by
Christa French

Advaita Press

Published in the USA by

Advaita Press
PO Box 3479
Redondo Beach, CA 90277
Tel: 310-376-9636
Email: fellowship@advaita.org
www.advaita.org

Cover Design : Louis Lefebvre

Rear Cover Photo: Gayle Goodrich

ISBN: 0-929448-21-9

Library of Congress Card Number: 2004093595

10-9-8-7-6-5-4-3-2-1

For the Men
&
For the Women
Ahh, the women
Who I have loved
And who have loved me
Who have borne my children
Who have held me to their breasts
And for All
That with grace and passion
Has made me know I am alive!

About the Cover

In 1987 when Ramesh Balsekar was brought to the U.S. he was taken to a restaurant where he ordered the house special—a potato baked in a shell of clay. With great fanfare the potato was rolled to the table. The waiter then produced a small silver mallet with which he tap-tap-tapped on the clay until it broke and the potato was revealed.

Ramesh commented that his Teaching was a similar process. He tap-tap-tapped with his conceptual hammer of "All there is is Consciousness" and there was no way to predict how many taps would be required.

CONTENTS

EDITOR'S NOTE

One of Wayne's favorite questions to ask a new visitor is, "How is it that you came here today?" It's a potent question because it opens the door to our story and any beliefs that we hold true. It is this story of "me" that Wayne gently pulls out from under us in order to guide us back to That, which is the Source of everything.

When I discovered Wayne, I had already met several individuals who professed to be teachers of Advaita. For me, though, Wayne was the only Teacher I had met whose words felt completely clean. I know that he can identify with that statement because he felt the same way the first time he listened to his guru, Ramesh Balsekar. It wasn't a mental thing or even a gut feeling; in fact, it was nothing—no thing.

I came to Wayne a seeker. I wanted enlightenment, and I wanted to be there to experience it. Surprise! Here lies the O'Henry twist to the seeker's story. As Wayne has said so many times, the Final Understanding (or enlightenment) is the dissolution of the "me" that claims to be seeking. So, there is no 'one' left to revel in the glory of achievement. To make matters worse, there was nothing "I" could do about it, about anything for that matter. "I" had never done anything. When the full implications of this statement are understood, even on an intellectual level, there is such a tremendous sense of freedom and relief.

It is said that the most compassionate thing one can do for another is to show them that there is no one suffering. This dismantling process might not feel compassionate to everyone. It's not an easy process; it can be quite painful and frustrating. Wayne dissects our stories, burns our bridges, answers our questions with questions and leaves us with nothing. He has no agenda, no practices or techniques and offers no lifeline to which we can cling. In truth, though, what could be more wonderful, more loving? To me, a good friend is someone who is honest with me, someone who knows that the best way isn't always the easiest. With that definition in mind, Wayne is the greatest friend anyone could have. He's also terrific to hug, although you may have to stand on your tiptoes to do so because he's rather tall.

Shortly after I started providing transcriptions of the talks for posting on the advaita.org website, Wayne wrote an e-mail to me and said that I should "start thinking about putting these into a book." It was a bit of a shock. At first, it seemed a monumental task, and I didn't know where to start. "I" didn't have to know. As the work progressed and the Teaching had its effect, it was seen more and more that "I" wasn't doing anything. It—and everything else—was being done through this body/mind organism named Christa.

As are all things with Wayne, it has been a glorious adventure to work with him on this book. It has been a labor of love, an honor and a blessing. As I typed the words I could hear Wayne's booming voice, see his eyes flash, hear his wonderful laugh, and I knew Self was speaking to Self.

Yes, Wayne, "*Who* knew?"

Never mind.

Christa French
February 2004

ACKNOWLEDGEMENTS

The editor would like to thank some of the many people who have been involved in the making of this book. Particular thanks go to:

Proofreaders: Donna Tonery. Todd Haydon, Catherine Asche, Jaki Scarcello

Cover Layout and design: Louis Lefebvre

Rear Cover Photo: Gayle Goodrich

Index construction: Sandy Charles of Little Oak Indexing.

Thanks to Leonard Cohen for his permission to use the wonderful description of a sage from his novel *Beautiful Losers*.

Thank you to Scott Atkinson for his loving presence and endurance during the many hours of typing, editing and proofing this manuscript.

And to the dance!

♋ ♋ ♋

WHAT IS A SAGE?

What is a sage? A sage is someone who has achieved a remote human possibility. It is impossible to say what that possibility is. I think it has something to do with the energy of love. Contact with this energy results in the exercise of a kind of balance in the chaos of existence. A sage does not dissolve the chaos; if he did, the world would have changed long ago. I do not think that a sage dissolves the chaos even for himself, for there is something arrogant and warlike in the notion of a man setting the universe in order. It is a kind of balance that is his glory. He rides the drifts like an escaped ski. His course is a caress of the hill. His track is a drawing of the snow in a moment of its particular arrangement with wind and rock. Something in him so loves the world that he gives himself to the laws of gravity and chance. Far from flying with the angels, he traces with the fidelity of a seismograph needle the state of the solid bloody landscape. His house is dangerous and finite, but he is at home in the world. He can love the shapes of human beings, the fine and twisted shapes of the heart. It is good to have among us such men, such balancing monsters of love.

Leonard Cohen

♋ ♋ ♋

ONE

When a glimmer of Understanding happens,
You have a cancer.
It will grow...
Relentlessly replacing you with itself
Until you are gone.

Ram Tzu

THE TEACHING

Prior to becoming an Advaita teacher, I spent most of my adult life as a businessman. My guru, Ramesh S. Balsekar, is a banker. He spent his entire working life in the Bank of India and finally retired as the president. I find it amusingly ironic that he gave me nothing to sell you: no techniques, no plans, no instructions, no promise that if you just do what I tell you, you are going to get what you want. What he did give me were these simple pointers to "what is." I offer them here to you as a gift.

The process that happens here—and it's a very organic process—is one in which the emphasis is always on examining and seeing what is truly functioning in this world. Most people have the sense that they are the authors of their existence. Nearly everyone believes they are responsible for the creation of their thoughts, feelings and actions. The honest questioning of this basic assumption often leads to profound insight.

Please keep in mind that there's no doctrine here. There's nothing you must learn or believe. It's a process of questioning and looking and seeing for your self. The insight that may come as a result of this process is not even something that can be quantified. If the insight could be quantified then I could simply tell you what it is, and you could then take this "quantifiable" knowledge and learn it. Regrettably, that is not possible.

The process of this examination is to look deeply into what is actually functioning, to inquire into what is the animating force for everything, including the human body/mind package that you consider yourself to be. The teaching invites you to ask, "What is this thing composed of? What is this thing truly?" The beauty of the Teaching is it doesn't give you the answer. There's no doctrine that says, "What you truly are is (fill in the blank)." Now, there *are* pointers in the Teaching. They are like conceptual guideposts. A statement may be made to the effect, "What we truly are is Consciousness. What we truly are is God. What we truly are is Source." Those statements point you in a direction to look for yourself. But even such fundamental statements of the Teaching are not the truth, are not to be taken as an *a priori* truth, but are rather to be deeply examined.

There was a wonderful teacher who died about twenty years ago by the name of Wei Wu Wei. He had a Chinese pen name, but he was actually an Irish aristocrat. He used a term I like very much: "apperception." The pointer of this term was to suggest perception without a perceiver, knowing without a knower. This apperception that he talked about is a knowing *beyond* the organism, a knowing that is Total. It's not a relative perception. The Christian scriptures talk about this as "the peace that surpasses all understanding." The minute you understand it, it's not the peace that surpasses all understanding any more; it's now the peace that you understand. We're talking about a peace that surpasses all relative knowing, so it is a peace that can coexist with whatever is happening in the manifest world. You can still have responses to things. You can still have likes and dislikes, preferences about how you would run things if you were in charge. But the underlying peace is the recognition that you are in fact *not* running things; everything that exists in this moment is the perfect functioning of the Universe, not some accomplishment or mistake on the part of either the Universe or you.

Of the numerous bizarre ideas in modern spirituality, probaby my least favorite is the notion that you bring your sickness on yourself. The suggestion is that when one's understanding is wider and more expansive then the sickness doesn't arise, or if it does, it is seen as irrelevant. We are told that all we have to do is "let go" or "see rightly" and all will be corrected. This means that if you're sick, you're an idiot. Not only are you sick, but you're spiritually flawed on top of it, which is a truly ugly notion.

What this Advaita teaching points to—*points to*—is that life and death happen; health and sickness happen. They come, they go, as part of this miraculous movement of the universe; they are part of the fabric of manifest existence. Bodies are created through which (what we call) health and sickness happen. In the acceptance of the underlying reality that it's all part of a perfect functioning, your resistance to what is happening eases and the suffering attendant to what is happening lessens. You still have all the same issues. You still have to deal with the problems in your life. However, without this feeling that what is happening is a flaw in the Universe, there is more strength, there is more energy, there are more internal resources to deal with whatever life brings. Sometimes what life brings is not pleasant. In fact, sometimes it is terrible, but what we call "suffering" is a result of the belief that what is happening *should not* be happening.

The acceptance that I'm talking about is not approval. It doesn't mean you are required to like what is happening or refrain from doing something to change it. The acceptance is that it exists, as it is now, as part of a larger functioning, and the return to health, should it occur, also exists as part of that larger functioning. So changes happen. That's the very fabric of the manifestation: health turns into sickness, sickness turns into health; there's continuous movement. That is the ebb and flow of the Universe. We can have a preference for one condition over the other, but when one over the other is deemed to be the only thing that *should* exist, then suffering is inevitable.

When I met my guru, Ramesh Balsekar, he was talking about how Consciousness is everything. He said that we are aspects of That; therefore, everything we do is in fact the happening of Consciousness—EVERYTHING. That made enormous sense to me. I could see how that really worked, and it explained everything that I needed explained. It was very satisfying. *Everything everyone is doing is always the functioning of Consciousness.* No problem.

I left the talk and went home. My five-year-old son was doing something I had told him fifteen times not to do; he was sitting there doing it again! I started yelling, "What the hell is the matter with you? I have told you fifteen times not to do that! God damn it, don't you ever listen to me? Go to your room!" So he toddled off to his room. He knew me well enough to be totally unfazed by my tirades. But I was left with the terrible feeling of, "Wait a minute. I just spent all this time with a Master who has opened up the very secrets of existence. I see it, I believe it, and I know that it's true. I know deep in my gut that what my son was doing was the action of Source right there in front of me, and my response was to punish him and to reinforce this notion in him that he was doing it, that he was responsible for it." I was completely disgusted with myself.

The next day I went back to the talks—Ramesh was talking every day at a home in the Hollywood Hills—and I confessed to Ramesh about my Advaitic lapse. "Ramesh, I feel terrible. I went home and forgot your teaching completely, totally. Everything went out the window the moment I was confronted with my son doing something I didn't like. I yelled at him and I completely forgot that his action was the functioning of Totality, not his egoic action." And Ramesh looked at me with this amazing expression of compassion—I like to think of it as compassion and not pity—and he said, "Wayne, your yelling at your son was part of the functioning of the same Totality. Your response was part of the same matrix of existence, you see. You leave yourself out." And we do, inevitably; that is the divine hypnosis. Even when we buy the whole package, even when we say, "Yes, I see it. I believe it. It's true. It's there," in the next moment, when the ego claims authorship, we will consider ourselves responsible and respond with guilt or pride.

Sometimes the Teaching does arise and cut off that involved sense; the recognition that everything truly is the functioning of Totality arises and cuts off that involvement by this "me." That is the end of the suffering, because the suffering is that involvement. People often think the negative response is the suffering, but that's not the case; that is simply a response by the organism. The action in the moment is simply in the moment. Suffering arises when the actions and reactions in the moment are extended in time, projected away from what is in the moment. The suffering is the thought, "I shouldn't have" and all the subsequent projections of what it's going to mean for ME and how it's going to affect ME.

Of course, even that "suffering" is divine. You are

not the source of those thoughts; they happen *through* the body/mind organism commonly referred to as "you." In the magnificent tapestry of existence everything is absolutely perfect. When (and if) the suffering ends, it will not be "your" doing. Nothing is "your" doing. Isn't that wonderful!

♋ ♋ ♋

THIS ADVAITA

This Advaita, as I talk about it, is not actually a philosophy because it does not hold any tenets. It is simply a collection of pointers and concepts, and it posits that none of them are true in an absolute sense. This teaching is not about conveying the truth. It is about prying away the limitations and misconceptions about how things are. And so it is a process rather than a body of truths. Its statements comprise a collection of tools.

The primary tool is that everything is Consciousness; everything is One. Or to be even more precise, Advaita, literally translated, means "not two." That's the essential pointer. It is not a truth. And a pointer is to be used to see what is in fact operative; to look within oneself to see what one's nature is. It is very much a process that, when it happens, is understood to be part of the natural flow of life.

So the Teaching as it is happening now in this moment is having its effect. If there's an authoring "me" present, it will say, "Look what I have done. I've thought, I've realized, I've seen and I've paid attention today, and thus I've earned these benefits and results." The understanding is that it is the Teaching itself that is having its way with you. It is the Teaching itself that is having an impact on you, by *its* force.

The sage's role is to raze the whole conceptual spiritual structure. It is, to quote Hafiz, "to take away those toys that bring you no joy." If you see a two-year-old with a sharp knife and you take it away from him, he's going to scream. As far as he's concerned, you've done him a great harm. "That was MY toy. I was having fun with that." Your preventing him from chopping off his leg is a compassionate act. However, the child doesn't see it as a compassionate act.

So, often the action of the sage is not seen as compassionate. If I had to define compassion, I would say that the compassion of the sage is total acceptance, which means you are accepted completely as you are in the moment. The sage accepts the disciple fully as he is. This acceptance is an underlying quality to every action by the sage. The action may be to take away the toys, to push the disciple into areas where the disciple isn't comfortable, or to ask difficult questions and not let up. So the disciple goes away unhappy. "How can this be compassion? I'm unhappy. He wasn't kind and gentle with me. I feel worse now then I did when I walked in and met him." It is compassionate for one reason: there is no personal agenda on the part of the sage. Every single act is compassionate because there is no "me" desiring something for itself as part of the action. This is truly the blessing of the sage.

TWO

What is mind? No matter!
What is matter? Never mind!

Bertrand Russell (quoting his grandmother)

THE WHOLENESS OF THE PRESENT MOMENT

The teaching I offer to you is about *this*—this present moment—which is all-inclusive. When I say it's all-inclusive, I mean simply that it includes *everything*. It even includes the distractions and the feeling of separation. Of course, we like the moments where there's connection and presence, but the Teaching points to the fact that both exist, and they are alternating phenomenal states that one experiences as part of this manifest world. If they can be experienced, they are part of what is manifest.

In moments of pure meditation or in the presence that sometimes arises in spiritual gatherings, we become aware of the moment because everything is very still. Then in daily life, we get busy with work and interpersonal relationships and our involvement in those things seems to promote the sense of separation. Unity and separation are alternating experiential states. What we call the Final Understanding is the removal of that which shifts between states. For the sage there is neither state, because the state of exquisite presence is, by its nature, dependent upon its counterpart of involvement. Neither state can exist without the other. So the state of the sage is not phenomenally experienced. We can't even legitimately call it a state because there is no separation whatsoever; therefore, there can be no union and no separation. There simply is Oneness.

The state of the sage is not the presence of exquisite connection with God that seekers experience; rather, it is the complete *absence* of either presence or absence. What that leaves is the flow of events in the moment, the experience of whatever is happening: joy, sorrow, happiness, sadness, frustration, contentment. All of the interdependent opposites function through the sage, because it's a human organism operating in duality, so it will experience the same dualistic opposites as any human organism. What is absent in the sage is the quality of involvement and separation, which is a secondary quality that is laid on top of "what is." There is either peace with all of "what is," or there is involvement, separation and antagonism with "what is," and those are the alternating states for most people. It is quite natural to prefer the presence of the unified state to the presence of the involved or separated state, but for the sage neither state exists.

The ultimate understanding encompasses the polaric opposites. It doesn't discount them or negate them; it absorbs them, so all the polaric opposites of the universe continue and are part of the whole. There *is* wholeness. The identification has shifted *to* the wholeness, and the duality exists *within* the wholeness as an aspect of the wholeness.

Most people experience wholeness as one side of the dualistic movement between the *experience* of unity and the *experience* of separation. What is actually known is not wholeness; rather, it is the *experience* of wholeness that is only half of the equation. The wholeness itself cannot be experienced because there is nothing *outside* of it. For any dualistic experience, there is the opposite side, the other point of experience against which it is known. From the standpoint of wholeness, there is *nothing* other than that—no opposite side—therefore it can't be known in relation to something else. That wholeness is the *essence* of the sage, not the *experience* of the sage.

♋ ♋ ♋

SPIRITUAL HANGOVERS

Sometimes after a spiritual experience of unity and connection ends and one is thrust back into involvement, there can be a sense of dislocation that could be called a spiritual hangover. What is absent in the integrated state and what is hung over when it's coming out of this state is what Ramesh calls the *thinking mind*. The thinking mind is that aspect of the human organism that *falsely* claims it is the source of the organism's thoughts, feelings and actions.

The pointer of this teaching is that it is Consciousness that is authoring all action and animating everything. It functions through these human instruments in the same way that it functions through trees, birds or waterfalls. Humans are structured so that when the life force flows through them they react in accordance with their programming. So, there are murderer organisms, saint organisms, mother organisms, father organisms, worker organisms, lazy organisms; all are created to perform different actions. There are dog organisms, squirrel organisms, fish organisms, each of which act according to their biological nature and their conditioning. Consciousness functions through everything.

Each human organism is genetically programmed to produce a broad range of actions and reactions. It has instincts and physical needs. The organism reacts organically to this programming. It needs air and will fight to get it. It needs water; it needs food; it needs warmth and shelter; it has a need for sex; it has a need for all kinds of things. The needs of the organism drive action, completely independent of any egoic "I." Your own investigation will reveal that the presence of an egoic "I" is not required in order for actions to happen.

It is the ego or thinking mind that falsely claims the functioning of Consciousness as "my" doing. It blusters and threatens, suggesting that if "I" am gone nothing will be done. Of course, that is ridiculous! That is clearly not the case. In the absence of this egoic "I," the whole universe is done.

♋ ♋ ♋

ALLOWING

Are you saying that seekers can never find the experience of unity they are searching for?

No. They can find what they are looking for, which is the *experience* of unity. They find it all the time. Then it goes—it must go—and then they find it again. What they can't find is the *unchanging* experience of unity because all experience is dualistic and thus changing.

You talked about this acceptance of the movement between the two experiences of absence and fulfillment. How much of it is a person's effort in allowing this to happen versus "grace"—some kind of energy that just makes it easy? Sometimes I feel that I'm more a beneficiary of grace than of my own efforts to get there.

What you're asking is best answered by looking at the one who claims they would allow, or the one who claims they would do something to bring about the desired result, and see if it is the one who acts. What drives a particular action, be it an active action like meditating or a passive action like allowing? We have to remember that allowing is an action. All too often allowing is somehow seen as being in another category when, in fact, it is not. The allowing is a passive action. The real question is, is he or she the *author* of the action? Clearly, the organism is the doer of the action, but is this allowing or doing a *self-authored action*?

For example, you have done something: You decided to come here, and you came here. So let's look at this decision to come here. How did that decision come about? We have to deconstruct the decision and question the most basic assumption, which is that "I" decided. So, how did "I" decide? What influences were there in the decision? You felt physically all right tonight; you felt well enough to come. The positive physical condition that allowed a positive decision to happen clearly is not in your control. This is something you were given, so to speak, as you alluded to earlier. You're the beneficiary of that healthy body that allowed the decision to come here. If you had diarrhea, you would not get in the car and come sit some place for an hour and a half where you would have to get up every five minutes and embarrass yourself. So, you have physical health. You had a condition handed to you that was a major component in your decision: you felt well.

Another factor is that there was an interest in the subject. If you had no interest in the subject, if you preferred to watch a television show such as "American Idol," then you would not have come here. The question is did you create this personality that is more interested in spirituality than "American Idol" or did it evolve as a result of certain factors in your life—educational, environmental, cultural—that influenced your spiritual interests and your eventual choice to come here? If we dissect it and look at the factors that were involved in the decision, things over which you had no input, it is clear that there is no question as to whether you were the creator. So, on what basis can you really claim authorship if the influences on the decision are outside your control?

I understand.

Okay. So, if there is no legitimate claim of authorship, then there are forces at work other than one's egoic self that bring about the decisions, the actions and the emotions. You use the word "grace," and that describes this sense of "it is happening as a result of forces greater than my egoic self, and the outcome is to my liking." We generally don't use the term "grace" when these forces outside of our control are perceived as disadvantageous—when we have cancer, when someone dear to us is struck tragically in an accident—even though it is the product of the same force that brought about the good stuff. We use the terms *grace* as a spiritual synonym for good luck and "God's will" to denote bad luck.

Now I happen to like the term "grace," and I use it often to describe events that happened in my life that I perceive as beneficial. The curious thing is that a lot of the things that happened that I now perceive as grace did not feel like grace at that time. I'll use a very dramatic example from my own life. For nineteen years, I was an alcoholic and drug addict. The last five or six years of my drinking and drug abuse things got serious and there were a lot of unpleasant physical repercussions. My ankles and wrists were swollen with alcoholic edema, and I was carrying a big wad of toilet paper in my pants that I was changing every twenty minutes because my bladder was leaking. I was clearly very sick, but I was in absolute denial that there was a problem.

At the end of the Memorial Day weekend and yet another three-day binge, I was lying in bed and I felt that obsession leave, an obsession that had compelled me to drink even when it was killing me. I felt it go. It had been with me for nineteen years, and suddenly it was absolutely gone. My reaction in that moment was terror mixed with resignation. I was not happy about this change. I clearly had no input into the event. It was obvious that this was something that had happened *to* me. I knew I was transformed in that moment, but my immediate reaction was, "This is not a good thing." The realization that I could not drink any more was horrific. My whole life was built around the bars, the people in the bars, the drug houses. I didn't like people who didn't drink and didn't use drugs; I never wanted anything to do with such people. Suddenly I *was* one of those people, and as far as I was concerned, this was a tragedy.

Though it did not seem so at the time, from where I sit today, I believe that was *utter* grace, *complete and total grace.* In fact, it was the moment when my spiritual seeking began, because I wanted to find out what the hell had happened to me. What power was there in the universe that could do such a thing to me? Prior to that, I had assumed I was the master of my destiny. This was irrefutable evidence that something could have a profound impact on me without my desiring it. It had clearly happened totally independent of my will.

So whenever the questions arise, "Is there something I can do? What can I do to make this better? How do I get what I want?" my answer is do whatever seems appropriate *knowing* that what is actually functioning is Source, and we and everything else are instruments of that functioning. The teaching says if there is a question at hand, do what you think is best in the moment. You say, "I don't know what's best. I'm in conflict. One day this seems right, the next day that seems right. I don't know what to do." Do what you feel is best in the moment. Then we will see what happens.

That's the practical aspect of it, but the underlying understanding of the Teaching always points back to the fact that the reason we are saying all this is because what is truly functioning—*always, always*—is Consciousness.

♋ ♋ ♋

CONSCIOUSNESS IS ALL

Everything is the functioning of Consciousness, because Consciousness is all there is. That's the fundamental pointer of the Teaching. Everything is Consciousness, thus, everything that happens is Consciousness.

But Consciousness is not some *thing* that can be absorbed by the human mind. When we use the word "Consciousness," we are not talking about a thing. If it were a thing, then it could be comprehended by the human mind; if it were an object, it could be known. In this teaching, the word "Consciousness" is used to point to *everything*—the source *and* the substance of everything—and, yet, it is not a thing, not an object. It can never be known in its entirety because there is no "it" to be known. Consciousness can only be known in its aspect, which is this entire manifest world.

♋ ♋ ♋

THREE

The world itself is a miracle. I am beyond miracles— I am absolutely normal. With me everything happens as it must. I do not interfere with creation. Of what use are small miracles to me when the greatest of miracles is happening all the time?

Nisargadatta Maharaj

INTELLECTUAL UNDERSTANDING

The intellectual understanding of the Teaching limits horizontal thinking. Is that correct?

It may arise and cut off involvement by the "me," which is what we may call "horizontal thinking."

Was that the case for you?

Yes, it frequently did as "the understanding deepened," which is a way of saying that this intellectual understanding would arise more often in more situations to cut off involvement. As the understanding deepened, there was less involvement.

So with the thought "I am not the author" the involvement lessens, which results in less suffering?

It isn't only the thought that "I am not the author," rather it is the awareness of "what is."

But the thought that "I am the author" is also part of Totality expressing itself.

Oh, absolutely.

So even a conflict that I feel because of that thought is Totality expressing itself?

Absolutely.

So if I continually say "I am not the author" then . . .

I am not talking about you doing anything. What I'm talking about is that when the understanding deepens and the thought arises, then the *understanding* cuts off the involvement. I am not talking about *you* applying an intellectual concept to a situation, as you would use a technique in order to get some desired result.

So the ego cannot learn the Teaching.

The ego cannot apply the Teaching. The ego is powerless.

How is the structure of the ego related to the structure of the body/mind organism?

The ego is a term that we use in several ways, so it can be confusing. My guru, Ramesh, has made a very precise distinction that helps clarify the matter. He took the ego or the mind and split it into two notions: the thinking mind and the working mind, or the thinking ego and the working ego. The working ego is that aspect of the body/mind mechanism that is the repository of genetic predisposition—your basic nature—and all of the subsequent conditioning of experience, learning, culture—everything that has happened to the organism up to this moment. It is what works, what thinks, what determines how you act. This working ego is dynamic; it is changing every instant.

The thinking mind or thinking ego is a sense that arises in every human at around the age of two-and-a-half. Its only function is to claim the output of the working mind as its own creation. The working mind is cogitating, acting, reacting. The thinking mind claims authorship and says, "*I* thought that. *I* felt that. *I* decided. *I* am the one who did all that." It is a false claim, but that false claim brings the "authorship" here to the body.

The simplest investigation will reveal that the organism did not produce its own genetic predisposition nor did it produce the vast quantity of conditioning of the organism. It couldn't possibly have done so. Yet, thinking mind, this thinking aspect of the ego, claims primacy. It says, "*I'm* the one who's deciding. *I'm* the one who's feeling. *I'm* the one who's thinking." And of course, the fear is, "What if *I* don't do it right? What if *I* screw up?" When things go badly, that's the guilt: "*I* didn't do it well. *I* could have done it differently, but *I* didn't."

So guilt and fear wouldn't rise up because they are based on a judgment.

They are based on a claim of personal authorship by *"me."* If my action is not sourced here, if I'm simply the instrument of the action, how can I be guilty? Is a knife used in a murder guilty of murder?

Well, there could be conditioning for guilt.

Guilt only has meaning if there is a belief that I am the source, I am the creator.

Let's say that the sage is playing chess and makes a bad move. Wouldn't there be a spontaneous arising in the moment, "I should have moved that piece," even if there would be no belief present that it could happen any other way?

Only linguistically. He might say, "That was a stupid move. I should have moved the other one." But there is no one there to believe he was the author of the move, therefore the sense of "should" simply doesn't arise. That's the pointer. So any example you come up with will always be answered with the same pointer: there is no authoring sense in the sage.

♋ ♋ ♋

AS YOU ARE

Why do people do nasty things? Isn't it because they are not conscious enough? Shouldn't they be doing self-inquiry or some other practice to raise their consciousness?

Well, why aren't they more conscious? If they could be more conscious, there would be more peace and contentment in their lives. Why doesn't everyone become more conscious and have more peace, when all they have to do is sincerely ask, "Who Am I?" All their problems would be over! Why don't they do that? What is inhibiting the sincere asking of that one question that unlocks this incredible bonanza? This is where the inquiry I'm talking about starts.

I'm flawed. I'm weak. I haven't done it well enough. That's why it hasn't worked.

Well, let's start there: What is it about the way you are constructed that inhibits you from doing what you intend? You may not be able to say what it is, but there is some thing in you that inhibits your ability to do what you would like and, obviously, it's not within your control to remove it; otherwise, you would have removed it a long time ago. So, there is some thing over which you have no control that inhibits your action; some thing is dictating what is happening. What is this?

It's a strongly held notion in society that you can be other than you are; however, it's a notion that bears examining. Certainly, you can be other than you were—meaning that you can change—but can you be other than what you are in the moment?

If you examine yourself, you may see that what you are in the moment is a product of a vast matrix of genetic and environmental forces. What you are in the moment is what acts, and what you are in the next moment may well act differently since environmental forces are constantly altering your matrix.

♋ ♋ ♋

PAIN

Ultimately, the understanding I am pointing to is an acceptance of "what is," whatever that may be in the moment. The acceptance of "what is" eliminates the suffering. It doesn't eliminate the pain. If pain is part of "what is," there is pain. It could be intense emotional pain or intense physical pain. Pain is an aspect of being alive; it comes with the mind and the body.

And the acceptance of "what is" is not so much of a passive acceptance, but it is more of an understanding that what is happening is the way it is supposed to happen through this one Consciousness?

"Supposed to happen" is one way of saying it. But specifically we are saying, "It is what it is!"

And the suffering comes in wanting it other than it is?

Yes. Or, more precisely, in feeling it *should* be other than it is. The desire to want the pain to go away is very natural, and the steps that follow to eliminate the pain are part of the organism. So wanting to change things in the future is quite benign. But if there is also the notion that "this should not be as it is," then that is the root of suffering.

♋ ♋ ♋

WHO WITNESSES?

Wayne, I want to ask you about the so-called "witness state." In this state, who is the witness?

It is impersonal. There is no "who" associated with it until afterwards, then you say, "*I* had that experience."

Yes, I see it; yes. During the witnessing, there is no real sense of who is witnessing, so afterwards it is the mind that seeks to pin down the "who."

Yes.

It's funny actually! It's a kind of farce, played out by one actor—the ego!

Yes, in a play written by Consciousness.

Yes!

The ego is the instrument through which Consciousness acts.

Why is it that the witnessing then seems to cease?

Because it is a phenomenal state and MUST change.

It's a stage in a process.

It is an event in phenomenality.

But so are a lot of other things that make up "daily life," such as sensations of taste, smell, and etcetera. I mean the climate is also an event.

Yes.

But it's always there.

The weather is always there and it is always changing. If it never changed, there would be nothing to notice.

♋ ♋ ♋

FOUR

Reality is merely an illusion, albeit a very persistent one.

Albert Einstein

SUFFERING

Many non-dual teachings start and end with the concept "you are That"—full stop—and anything else is dismissed as illusion and ignored. You are God; you are Source—period. It's purely a matter of personal taste, but I like to start with what is apparently manifest. That's where all the juice is; that's where life is happening. All the drama is in this apparent separation, and it is both miraculous and fascinating. I prefer to start with where you apparently are, then move back to pointing to the Source.

Ultimately, you come full circle back to "what is," because "what is" is Source manifest. There is an *appearance* of separation, peopled by organisms interacting as if they were independent entities, and that creates an extraordinary drama. That's entertainment; that's fun. Admittedly, sometimes it's incredibly tragic entertainment. It can be excruciating, but the flipside of excruciation is an immense pleasure and joy.

Some of what happens in life we experience as crap. But when you look deeper into it, the crap may be the product of a gloriously beautiful and delicious meal. When it is dug back into the ground, it may then be the fuel for the production of a beautiful and delicious vegetable that you eat, and then it turns back into crap again. You have crap, but along with the crap, you have wonderful things. They arise together. If you have crap, you have incredible joy and beauty. They're not separate; they're different points on the same circle. You can tell when you've been poked in the eye or when you've been lovingly stroked. There's a difference between pleasure and pain in experiential terms. When we say that they're the same, obviously, they're not experienced as the same, but we are saying they have the same root. They are twin aspects of the same thing.

Part of life and living is having preferences. Most people prefer pleasure to pain, unless they're masochists and then the pain is the pleasure and it gets a bit convoluted. The fact is that the organism has a preference in accordance with its nature. There is no inherent problem with the preference. Suffering arises when there is a sense that the pain *should not* be there, that the ugliness *should not* exist, that existence is fundamentally flawed, or that somehow the universe made a mistake. Suffering isn't caused by your not liking something; liking and not liking is part of "what is." It's the sense that "what is" *should not* be that is the source of suffering.

♋ ♋ ♋

If you are not going to change your route,
Why change your guide?

Antonio Porchia

♋ ♋ ♋

WHY TEACH?

Since I often start my Talks with the admonition that what I am about to say is not the Truth, people frequently follow that up with the question: So why do you teach?

In short, "I" do not teach. The teaching is expressed without any personal agenda. The expression may come forth as a result of a question from someone, or it may come forth as a burst of creative energy, as in the case of spontaneous poetry or these lines you are reading now. What is absent is the slightest shred of belief that what is being said or being written or being thought is the Truth. Any expression is understood at the most fundamental level to be a pointer, a relative teaching tool.

That's why the sage is said to have a natural humility, because there is the total absence of the conviction that what is being expressed is the Truth. The humility comes from the deepest possible conviction that what is being expressed is relative.

So, I personally have no trouble with anybody else's teaching. If one teacher says that you exist and another one says you don't exist, and this one says that you're God incarnate and this other one says that you're nothing, I don't care. They are all understood to be relative teaching tools. There is never a question of the hammer being Truer than the screwdriver. What I find objectionable (in an aesthetic sense) is when someone says, "What I am saying is the Truth and what the other teaching is saying is bullshit." Such an assertion lacks the essential clarity of understanding that it's all bullshit, and that a given teacher's teaching is a matter of enculturation and personal programming that determine how their teaching is expressed.

As you navigate the shifting reefs and shoals of the spiritual sea it may be useful to remember that that which is the most solid is also the most likely to sink you.

♋ ♋ ♋

ULTIMATE UNDERSTANDING

Ultimate understanding is an event, not a state. This thing that we call the final understanding is the death of the false belief that I am a discrete object with the powers of God, that I create my destiny, that I am the source of my thoughts, feelings and actions. That belief falls away, but it is not replaced with another, more expansive belief, such as, what I truly am is Source. The false sense of separation simply is no longer there.

So, what remains is an organism with qualities and characteristics—with a personality. As a human being, that organism has happy days and sad days, pleasurable days and painful days. There is the absence of suffering in that organism because it is the belief in its primacy as a separate object that creates the suffering. In the absence of that suffering, we can say there is peace. However, it isn't the peace that is conditional; it isn't the peace that changes, which moves from disquiet to peace. Rather, as the Christian scriptures talk about it, it is "peace that surpasses all understanding." It is a peace that is not conditional. It is a peace that underlies all of the responses of the organism. So the organism can be angry, miserable, disappointed, terrified; it can have all of these responses, and still underneath these responses is this peace that surpasses all understanding.

Now, viewed from outside, people say, "I want that,"

but viewed from the inside, the sage does not *have* it. The sage does not experience possessing it because the sage IS it. So, when you ask, "What is the point of this understanding," generally, what you're asking is, "What is the benefit for "me" in getting the understanding?" I would say that the benefit for "you" in getting the understanding is zero. There is absolutely no benefit for "you" in gaining the understanding, because when the understanding is gained, the "you" is gone.

Sages have tried in a variety of ways to point to the fact that there is no longer an egoic identification with the dualistic experience of the organism. The sage Nisargadatta Maharaj used to make statements such as, "I am awake even when I am asleep. I was never born, nor shall I ever die." Why? He was talking from the point of view of Consciousness, which is what we truly are. He was saying what we *are* never was born and never dies, is always present, is constant, and is without desire.

Interestingly, what people hear is that the sage has no desires; the sage doesn't sleep like the rest of humanity; the sage is some sort of super-being that never was born and never will die. They hear this because they are relating these statements to the organism, but the whole point is that it is NOT the organism. You are not limited to this organism. You are Consciousness. The sage will say, "I am That." What people hear is that this piece of meat knows the Truth, but that is not what is being said. It's not being spoken from the point of view of the meat. The meat cannot know its true nature; the meat is meat. The meat was born, it will die, it will have spiritual experiences and it will sleep when it sleeps. But even though the meat is dualistic and transient, the sage reminds us that the true nature of the meat *is* Consciousness.

The organism we call the sage has its innate imperatives: it seeks air; it seeks food; it seeks water; it seeks companionship; it seeks sex; it seeks love; it seeks pleasure; it seeks all manner of things in accordance with its structure and programming. However, in the sage there is no additional quality in that seeking; there is no fundamental emptiness at the heart of the seeking. The seeking is only for that which is sought, not to satisfy something missing—fundamentally missing—which is why most people seek things. Most people seek to feel complete, to feel fulfilled, and that does not happen for a sage.

In the cases of genuine understanding, the result is, more often than not, a response to living that is completely ordinary. The spiritual awakenings or experiences that happen to seekers are extraordinary. What characterizes these events is "someone" for whom this profound event and incredible insight has happened. That kind of event is transient . . . powerful, dramatic, potent, exciting, amazing, and insightful, but still transient. The event that creates the sage is simply the falling away of a false notion. *Nothing* has changed. The universe is *exactly* as it has always has been, because what is "revealed" is that there *never* was a separate "me." The sense that "I" was separate was never true.

Imagine you're being hypnotized and the hypnotic suggestion is that your clothes are on fire. If you're hypnotized to believe your clothes are on fire, when you look down what you'll see is your clothes on fire. You'll make efforts; you'll do things to make the fire go away. When the hypnotist snaps his fingers and says, "Wake up!" not only will you see there's no fire, but in this waking up you will also simultaneously understand that there *never* was any fire. The fire was completely illusory. So all the questions about the fire, such as what happened to the fire or how was the fire removed, are rendered irrelevant. There's no great revelation that there never was a fire. There simply never was a fire.

For the seeker, the knowledge that there is no fire can be quite beneficial. Even though he may look down and see fire, the understanding that it is not what it appears can cut off the involvement. The absence of involvement brings you *here,* into the moment, which is what I would call acceptance. The Teaching can be instrumental in bringing that about. When it happens, you would say that's one of the benefits of the Teaching. The organism we call the sage literally has no such knowledge. The sage is completely present with what is happening. That shift of perspective that cuts off the involvement is not present in the sage. Since there is no involvement, there is no separate perspective necessary or even possible in the sage. There's no need to bring about what already is total, complete acceptance all of the time. The acceptance is total because that which would accept is no longer present. Therefore, the movement in and out of acceptance is no longer possible. It is acceptance without an acceptor. For the seeker there is acceptance, which is then claimed by an acceptor, and that state comes and goes, or as Ramesh calls it, "flips and flops." As long as there is a "me" getting involved, then there is flipping and flopping in and out of that experience of acceptance.

When the enlightenment happens, *there is no one who is enlightened*. So there isn't someone thinking, "Ah, this is a major event that I finally got this enlightenment that only a small percentage of seekers get." The whole paradigm becomes moot. It isn't that all of a sudden the fire is gone; there was never a fire! 'What is' is simple and clear.

Generally, the energy behind seeking is to get "that," and the belief is that when "I" get "there" it will look a certain way, so it's understandable that questions arise from seekers about the landscape of enlightenment. The source of the interest is in learning how it is going to be if "I" get to be one of the special ones. What is it going to be like for "me?" So, where do you start? You start with someone for whom that has happened. You ask, "What's it like?" You try to gain some clues as to what it will be like for "me" when "I" get it. That's completely understandable. But my point again—and always—is "you" don't get it.

♋ ♋ ♋

If your house is built on quicksand,
does it make any sense to build another story?
Wayne

♋ ♋ ♋

ACCEPTANCE

Whenever we talk about acceptance one important point must be kept in mind: acceptance does not mean approval. Acceptance underlies the response. Thus, there can be anger, there can be frustration, there can be impatience, and there can still be acceptance. The acceptance underlies "what is." Anger, when it arises, is part of "what is," frustration, when it arises, is part of "what is." The acceptance is of everything; it is total. Likes and dislikes, approval and disapproval are aspects of each human organism. They arise naturally and spontaneously in accordance with the nature of each person, and a sage is no exception. That organism we call a sage is a human being with human qualities and characteristics.

The sage has likes and dislikes and, as is the case with everyone, the responses are automatic. Everyone's responses are a result of their conditioning. The ordinary person has an ego that claims the response and says, "I did it." The sage has no secondary claim about the natural response of the organism. That's the difference. But the process is the same for everybody. Every organism acts out of its conditioning. Every organism acts out of its nature.

What is absent in the sage is the arising of guilt and pride. Guilt cannot arise where there is no claiming of the action as being sourced by "me." That's what guilt and pride are: a false claim by the "me" of personal authorship.

FIVE

Chuang Tzu dreamed that he was a butterfly.
When he awoke, Chuang Tzu became confused.
"Am I a Man," he thought, "who dreamed that I was a butterfly?
Or am I a butterfly, dreaming that I am a man?"

LIFE IS BUT A DREAM

The classic Advaita pointer that this manifest universe has no more reality than a dream is one of the most misinterpreted. I believe that the original pointer was to the fact that in this apparent universe, each object appears separate and independent, and it is that independence of objects that is like a dream, not the appearance itself, but the appearance as separate independent entities. The basic Advaita pointer is that everything is Consciousness. Therefore, each thing that appears discrete is in fact an aspect of Consciousness and is in no way independent of Consciousness.

That's where this teaching tool that this is all a dream is meant to point. If you look around, it appears that a dog is different from a chair, a clock is different from a tree; each is an independent object. Their connection one to the other is not readily apparent. Everything *appears* separate and independent. But that's only an appearance, as in a dream, where everything appears real but has no existence independent of the dreamer. So the illusion is dreamlike in its nature because of this *appearance* of separateness that is not the actual state of things. The actual underlying reality is that everything is One.

When I say everything is an aspect of the One, I'm not suggesting that your perception of things should be any different. The perceiving apparatus is structured so that it sees things discretely. The way the eyes register things is that light bounces off a particular object, it reflects onto the retina, and a portion of the brain records that image. Those impulses together form an image that is an object. Because of the very structure of the way that the perceiving apparatus works, it does identify things as separate objects. So to suggest that you try and perceive differently is silly and unnecessary.

What the Teaching is pointing to is that this appearance is part of the whole manifestation. The fact that things appear separate to you is how the universe is constructed. This isn't a mistake on your part that you can't see the unity of things. *We are objects created to see the separation.* That's how we function in the world, and if you can't distinguish between the different qualities of the different objects, you can't function. Distinctions are necessary so that you know what is food and what is shit; which is your house and which is the gas station.

So when we say every object is an aspect of the Whole, this isn't something that is verifiable by the perception, nor is it the physical experience of the so-called enlightened human being—the sage. The sage functions completely as a human apparatus with all of its conditioning, qualities and characteristics, and it perceives in accordance with those. What is absent in the sage is the belief that each of these objects is an independent *creative* force. And *nothing* replaces that belief. It isn't replaced by the belief that all of these objects are aspects of the whole. That pointer is merely for teaching purposes and is used when somebody asks about the structure of things. The nature of the sage is to directly respond in the moment to whatever is happening.

♋ ♋ ♋

Do you believe in free will?
"Of course, I have no choice."
Isaac Bashevis Singer

♋ ♋ ♋

THE MYTH OF ENLIGHTENMENT

In my definition, enlightenment is an event that happens through a human being.

Since enlightenment is not a condition that someone has, but rather an event that occurs, you may have to completely rethink this whole notion of enlightenment. The defining quality or characteristic of that event is that the whole interest in and pursuit of enlightenment becomes moot. It is revealed that the attainment of enlightenment (which is being sought so that "I" can be enlightened) is impossible.

Some eight or ten months after the event happened through me, I was in India talking with Ramesh about how the whole question of enlightenment was moot and the language of talking about it was awkward. I said to him "So if someone asks me, 'Are you enlightened?' I would have to say, 'No'" (for the very reason I just articulated—that there's no one who is enlightened). And his response was, "You would have to say, 'No, but there is understanding or enlightenment *here*.'" And the *here* is not in the meat. The *here* is in this presence, in this moment. In *this*. Ramesh gave such a beautiful pointer.

That event was a moment in the history of the organism named Wayne in which that belief in personal authorship that I had since the age of two-and-a-half disappeared. By personal authorship, I mean that I, as this body/mind organism, am the source of my thoughts, feelings and actions. That belief was in an instant revealed as a chimera, as non-substantial, like a hypnotic suggestion that gets removed when the hypnotist snaps his fingers. That hypnotic suggestion was never real. You believed it was real, but it was never real. So when this false belief is revealed as not being true, nothing has changed. It was *never* true. And it is still not true.

♋ ♋ ♋

WHAT IS

If everything is meant to be, do you find yourself ever saying something like, "Well, it's meant to be. That's the way it is?"

Actually, there is a subtle difference between "the way it is" and "the way it's meant to be." Saying things are the way they are meant to be is one of the stories we tell about "what is." The pointer of this teaching is that the entire matrix of existence—everything that ever was, ever could be or will be—arose at once. What is, is. That's the pointer. It IS. The way the *is-ness* is experienced is in sequence, in duration. Thus, from the personal perspective, it can be conceptualized as being "predestined" or "the way it's meant to be," but the real essence of the understanding is that all that is, is—ALL of it IS.

Whether it seems to be or not, it is. It's just the way it is.

Not *just* the way it is, it IS.

If a situation happens, whether I interact with it and change it or not interact with it, it still is? Whether it's right, wrong, good, bad, whatever, it still is?

Yes, everything that happens is part of what is. So perhaps you can begin to look into the nature of this "doing" to change it. How does that doing arise? Are you the source of the doing that changes it? Or are you the *instrument* of the doing that changes it? We always come back to these essential questions.

That means the Source is driving the change. Isn't that the ultimate cop out?

It often is described that way. The last refuge of the ego is the threat: "By disempowering me, you're abdicating responsibility!" But that presumes you had the responsibility to abdicate in the first place. The understanding of the Teaching is that the responsibility was never yours. You will act responsibly or irresponsibly in accordance with your nature in the moment. Some people hear the Teaching and filter it through that most basic of presumptions: the presumption of personal authorship. The ego then simply rejects the notion without even examining it. It says, "That's crap, absolute crap. I'm in charge here. No one can tell me differently." The whole question is dismissed without even looking at it, which is simply another way to avoid the inquiry.

This teaching has no doctrine. The teaching may say Source does everything, but only as a pointer, not as a doctrinal Truth. What the Teaching is really saying is, "You look!" And after you've looked, after you've done the investigation, see what happens; see what the inquiry produces. I have yet to find anyone who has engaged in this process of investigation who has come up with a satisfactory example of an authoring "me" with any power. I've been at this for a long time, and a lot of people have attempted it. It could happen. I'm ready. I'm open to being shown such an entity, but so far, that Grail remains elusive.

♋ ♋ ♋

QUESTIONS

Prior to being exposed to this teaching, I was not aware that I had the conviction that I was the author of my thoughts, feelings and actions. It was simply taken for granted as an *a priori* truth. But as I was exposed through Ramesh to this teaching, I began to look for myself and see that was a very basic assumption: I had a very firm but unexamined belief that I was the master of my destiny.

As this inquiry progressed, I started to see more deeply. Clearly, if I could control my actions, if I could control my thoughts, my life would be more to my liking. I would never hurt people. I would never say nasty, stupid things. If I were in control, I'd never be hurtful. I find no benefit in hurting anybody. I've observed that when you're nice to people, they tend to be nice back to you. The more generous you are with the universe, the more that seems to flow back. These are principles I've observed over and over again, and, yet, I observed my actions being mean-spirited and nasty sometimes despite all of this brilliant awareness as to the way that the universe works and how it would be better for me if I didn't do those things. I did them anyway.

It became apparent that I was not fully in control. So once that point was established then the question was, "How much in control am I?" Did I really choose to be born with the IQ that I have? If so, why aren't I smarter? Did I choose to be born with the nature that I have? If so, why aren't I nicer? Did I choose to be born into the socio-economic level that I have? If so, why aren't I richer? What is the source of my actions? What is the source of my thoughts? What is the source of my feelings? Is it local, within the organism? Is the source here, within my body/mind mechanism? Or is this an object with a human name, an instrument through which these doings happen?

Those were the questions. And this teaching did not provide a doctrinal answer to the questions. The teaching simply asked the questions—persistently asked the questions. As I looked into the questions, the understanding gradually deepened. There was continuing insight, and more and more this understanding would arise and cut off whatever it was I'd be involved in. And what I found was that the less involvement that there was, the greater the peace.

♋ ♋ ♋

CONFUSION

In the middle place, between convictions, is where the confusion lies. If you can survive in the middle place, you survive in confusion. What the Teaching does is throw a lifeline to you and say, "follow this to some kind of sanity; follow this to some kind of peace."

Whether or not you can grab it, whether or not you

can hold on to it, or whether or not you can follow it, is another matter entirely. But that's what the Teaching throws to you. . .

As always, we will see what happens.

♋ ♋ ♋

KARMA

I'm not schooled in karmic philosophy but Ramesh has often said that karma is simply another word for "cause and effect." I prefer a scientific approach to karma, which is to say that we know that these organisms are affected by genetics and, thus, karma is transferred in the genetics. Each life is the result of untold past lives—lives lived through millions of prior births that have combined genetically and then transferred into the current organism. Where the notion of karma gets confusing is in the idea of *my* previous births. Who is this "me" that had the previous births? That is the crux of the question. Yes, there were previous births, clearly, and the influence on the current organism through the genetic legacy is unquestioned. But where does the "me" fit into the picture?

You're probably familiar with the great sage of Arunachala, Ramana Maharshi. This was the crux of his question: Who is this "I" that claims previous births? What is the nature of that "I?" Is it this body/mind? If it is not this, what is it? His pointer was to find out who you truly are. Once you determine what "you" are now, what you were in previous births is revealed.

♋ ♋ ♋

SIX

Wisdom sets bounds even to knowledge.
Friedrich Nietzsche

RESONANCE

I find it fascinating how we end up attracted to a particular spiritual teacher or teaching. When I met my guru Ramesh I wasn't looking for a guru and yet I found myself falling helplessly in love with this little Indian banker. I kept asking myself, "What the hell is going on here?" I was drawn to him again and again, simply to be in his presence, to be of service to him, to somehow be connected to him. All of that arose in me and yet it had never been characteristic of me. When I told my friends about Ramesh, how great he was, and how extraordinary the experience of being in his presence, they went up to see him with me. Their reaction was, "Nice little Indian guy you've got there. I hope you're very happy together. Let us know how it turns out." That was so astounding because for me there was the experience of the Guru—a palpable experience of Presence. This other person is sitting right next to me in the same room in the same moment and is clearly not experiencing that. What he's experiencing is a very nice man who says some very sensible things and seems just fine, but for him there's no

Guru there. So, in frustration at how this could be, I began to think about it a little more. Over the years, this scene was repeated time and again. Thus, this description of resonance seemed to fit this condition.

I describe resonance as a connection between two objects. In this model, the disciple-object is always a human being. The object at the other end of the resonant equation may be a person, or it may be an inanimate object, like a mountain. There's a very famous case where a mountain was the guru-object for a disciple named Ramana Maharshi. In this case, for Ramana, seeing, being near, or envisioning this guru-object Arunachala gave him a palpable experience of the Guru—Presence, Totality, God—whatever you want to call it. It was experiential for him.

Now in this model, when there is resonance between these two objects, the Guru is made manifest *out of* the resonance. The Guru—with a capital G—is made experiential for the disciple out of the resonance. When there is a guru-object at the other end of the resonant equation, be it human or inanimate, the experience of the disciple is to say, "When I am with him (or it) I experience Guru, therefore that guru-object is Guru."

We talk about it in those terms because that is the nature of the experience. It is like the way we talk about there being a sunset tonight, despite the fact that the sun is actually not moving. The sun is quite stationary in relation to us, but we still experience and talk about that event as the sunset. So, even though we understand that it is the resonance that produces the Guru experience, not the guru-object, we may still talk about the guru-object as the Guru. By understanding how it is the resonance rather than the other object that produces the experience, we can see how one person can come to the same guru-object with which someone else has resonance and not experience this same resonance or Guru. What you have in the absence of the resonance are simply two independent objects.

The resonance is experienced solely by the disciple. The disciple has the experience of the Guru. The human guru (the human object that may well be at the other end of the resonant equation) experiences the resonance only as it is reflected off the disciple. It's wonderful to be in the presence of the devotion, love and openness that arise out of that resonant connection. It's a joy for all people, not just the guru. Everyone is enriched who comes in contact with it.

When the human guru-object knows itself not to be the source of the resonance, the whole exchange is without further involvement. However, it sometimes gets quite ugly when the human object at the other end of that resonant equation sees the disciples sitting there, recognizes that what they are seeing is God, and thinks, "They're looking at me and they're seeing God. Clearly then, ipso facto, I must be God." It's at that point you don't want to drink the Kool-Aid. The ego, when it's present, inflates with the notion that "I," as the ego, am God and such involvement is never pretty.

SPIRITUAL EXPERIENCE

Often people are attracted to spiritual seeking after having an experience of Oneness. The diagram below is a model that describes the structure of this experience—

an experience that is sometimes mistaken for awakening. In it, the involved individual is going along in life and then there is a moment when the sense of being a separate egoic entity falls away. Life and living go on but without any sense of "me" to personalize this life and living. Life and living continues impersonally—happening perfectly—as part of the grand functioning of Totality. Then the individual "me" reemerges and says, "That was It. That was Truth. That was how things *should* be. I want that back." But "that" is the absence of the "me" that wants it back!

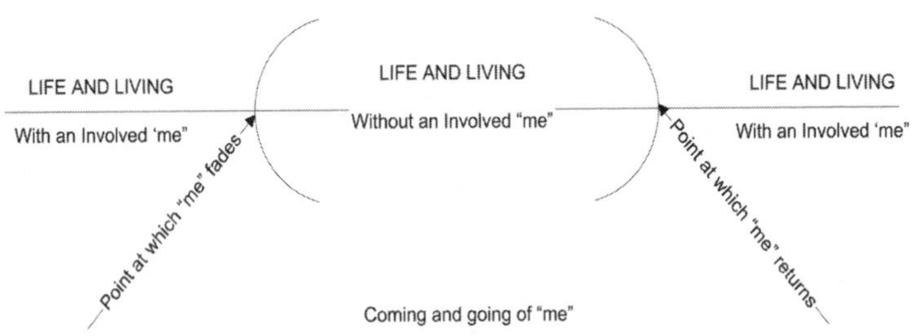

There is another aspect of this that gets really interesting. The space between the "me" falling away and the "me" coming back—that presence—is dependent on the "me" for it to be quantified as something that can be experienced. The brackets created from the "me" leaving and returning is what quantifies this presence as a *thing* that can be experienced and known. Now, for the sage this is what happens: The organism we call the sage is going along and this sense of "me" as the separate author is obliterated, irrevocably dead and gone. Life and living continue, but there is no "me" to come back and quantify this presence as something. Therefore, the sage does not experience that presence in the way that you know it, because what you know has been quantified as something by the "you" that has come back. The sage IS that presence. The sage does not *know* that presence, does not *experience* that presence as presence, because that "me" which would come back and quantify it has been obliterated.

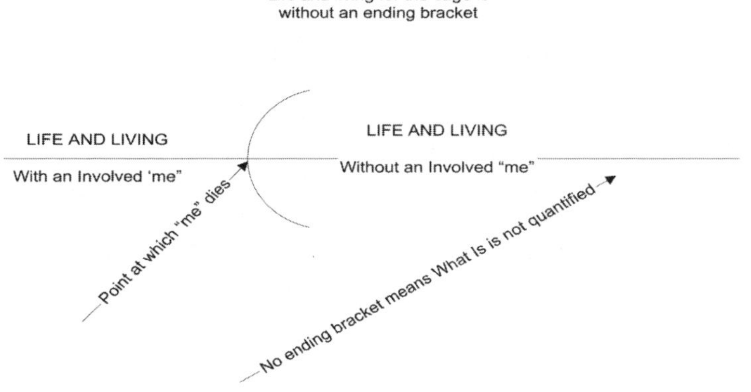

POWERLESSNESS

There is often a very strong negative reaction to the notion of powerlessness by the very same ego-structure that falsely claims the power. It's threatened. This teaching really does not have dogma. It doesn't hold as a tenet that there is no free will or that everything is predetermined. However, that conclusion is often drawn after undertaking the investigation that the Teaching suggests.

The teaching says, "Look for yourself. Examine your actions. If you're really in control, can't you do any better than this? If you really are in control, if you really have the power to make it happen, then why all the imperfection? Why are you not kinder, more generous, and more open?" You say, "Well, there must be some limitation to control." But if there's a limitation to the control, then we're having an interesting semantic discussion as to what about it is free. The teaching points to the investigation, whether it's Ramana's query, "Who am I? Who wants to know?" or Ramesh's, "Who's the doer? What is the source of the action?"

What is often revealed in the investigation is that the ego has no power; it is not the source it pretends to be. This insight often serves to weaken the claim of the ego. It isn't a question of whether or not the ego wants to weaken itself. The question is, "Does Totality want the ego to be weakened?" If it is part of this functioning of Totality that the ego be weakened, then there may be an attraction to this teaching and an undertaking of the investigation that shines a bright light onto the presumption of the ego.

There is a scene in the movie *The Wizard of Oz:* The protagonist, Dorothy, finally reaches the home of the Wizard she is seeking. When the curtain is thrown back, the Wizard is revealed as a little man operating levers; there's no Wizard there, really. That's what the Teaching does: it throws back the curtain. It doesn't throw it back very often or in very many cases, because most people aren't the slightest bit interested in pursuing it; most people haven't even a vague interest in doing so. Even the interest has to be given. You can't manufacture the interest for yourself or for others.

♋ ♋ ♋

ORIGINAL SIN

I was talking today with a man who told me, "Everything good in my life is a result of God. Everything bad in my life is a result of my action." He believes that all the good is God and all the bad is "me." In any other context, this would be considered a self-esteem issue, but it's a very common "spiritual" notion. It's the basis of original sin. The Catholics institutionalized this notion. Original sin: You are flawed from the moment of conception.

I do not believe we are flawed creatures. When I look around, what I see is a perfect universe. Some places I look it is beautifully perfect. Other places the perfection is unbearably ugly and painful. As a discriminating being, I prefer beauty to ugliness, pleasure to pain, joy to sorrow. But all are understood to be aspects of the same Source.

♋ ♋ ♋

SEVEN

A man can do what he wants, but not want what he wants.
Arthur Schopenhauer

WITNESSING

The awareness of a thought rising up, without a "me" watching the thought rising up, isn't that from an impersonal perspective?

In the moment that is happening, yes. As soon as there is the sense that "I" am having this experience, it's personalized.

And that occurs a split-second afterwards. That's the attachment, the reflex of the self, "That's mine."

That's right.

When coming from an impersonal perspective, those thoughts could rise up but they're not owned.

Yes, of course. There is impersonal awareness.

I watch my thoughts to see when there's a feeling of ownership, and when they rise up and, like a bubble, just go back. I'm curious as to what makes the grip, what makes the experience?

What is witnessed by you, what is seen by you as an impersonal experience, was an impersonal awareness that is subsequently personalized. So, it becomes "my" seeing of the impersonal arising. Since it was impersonal, the suggestion is that "I" am experiencing the impersonal. But that is a subsequent personalization of the impersonal.

That's where there's confusion: the hypnosis.

No. What we call the divine hypnosis is the existence of the authoring "me."

The desire for that impersonal experience is the hypnosis?

No. It is the *one* that would have the desire, not the desire itself. The divine hypnosis creates the one who is the conduit of the desire.

Whether it's experiencing a movie or experiencing enlightenment, isn't it all an experience thing—the psychosomatic organism wanting to claim and hold it, own it?

It gets even more complicated when we really dissect it, because there is an aspect of the personal that is not involved with the divine hypnosis. In order to point to this, Ramesh developed a concept he called the working mind and thinking mind process. He said there is an aspect of the personal that he calls the working mind. It's self-referencing; it knows its name; it knows when it is watching a movie; it can make airline reservations for itself; it knows where to put the food when "I" am hungry; it knows the food needs to go in my mouth, rather than in the flowerpot. It knows all these things because there's separation and personalization. All of that functioning—

which is identification with the name and form as a separate entity—must exist and must operate if the organism is to function in duality. What he calls the thinking mind is a subsequent occurrence, which is the sense of "me" as an egoic, authoring being. This quality claims the operations of the working mind as its creation. This "me" that's identified with the name and form proclaims itself as a creative force that authors the thoughts, actions or feelings of the organism.

I make this distinction between doership and authorship just to point clearly to this very separation, which is crucial in understanding what's going on from an intellectual position. It is the sense of authorship that disappears in the awakening—simply that.

And it can't dismantle itself.

It is a *false* claimer! It can't dismantle itself because it has *no power whatsoever* except to falsely claim credit for what happens through the organism, or to take blame for what doesn't happen.

The whole thing is Consciousness wanting to experience duality?

That's one way to talk about Consciousness that makes it friendly and human so that you can believe you know what it is. You say, "Well, the reason this is happening is because Consciousness is like a big person. 'He' is doing all of this creative stuff for a very human reason: because he wants to experience something or because it's interesting, or because it's lively," or for some other reason that makes sense from the human perspective. Then it's all tied up in a neat package. But the Consciousness we're pointing to is not an object, much less a person. It's literally not a *thing*. It's not a huge, powerful, authoring object called Consciousness. We talk about it that way. Our language suggests such imagery, but we have to constantly take the legs out from under that image and repeat over and over that this Consciousness is not a thing.

♋ ♋ ♋

BEING "IN THE NOW"

We are always in the now; there's no other place to be. Thought occurs in the now, so thinking is in the now. What is normally referred to as not being in the now is that involved, egoic process that projects into the past and the future. What's important to understand is that even when we're talking about that process, it's occurring in the now as part of what is.

If you're a seeker, you don't want to not be in the now. You've learned that it's a problem and you seek to eliminate it. Mind you, most people are not alert to the fact that this is a problem, and they go through their life blissfully unaware they are not in the now. But the seeker has investigated and seen that the source of suffering is this projection out of the moment. "Aha, I've identified what is the source of the suffering; now "I" will go about eliminating it." It's really an amusing concept when you break it down.

"I realize I don't exist as an authoring entity.

It is my belief that I exist as an authoring entity that is the whole problem.

Therefore, I (presumably as an authoring entity) am going to eliminate this."

Do you see the loop?

It is worthwhile to note that this involvement doesn't occur all the time. Every person goes through most of his or her life without that involvement. Ninety percent or more of what is experienced is without that horizontal involvement by the "me." But the horizontal involvement by the "me" is so powerful, so dramatic, and the source of so much suffering, that it is assumed to be always present.

♋ ♋ ♋

PEACE & HARMONY IN DAILY LIVING

This desire for enlightenment often causes more misery than happiness. Since enlightenment is not attainable by an individual, the frustration of years of trying to attain it causes a lot of grief. Yet, the effect of the Teaching is such that some people get more peace of mind, more ease in their day, and that could be considered a greater blessing than the concept of enlightenment.

In fact, Ramesh's book, *Peace and Harmony in Daily Living,* is devoted to saying essentially that: the measurable effect of the Teaching, and what most people are seeking, is peace and harmony in daily living. The man to whom he dedicated this book was a very successful Swedish lawyer who had reached the pinnacle of his profession in his country. He had everything he could possibly want in terms of prestige, money, recognition, and he was at Ramesh's because he still was not satisfied.

As this man described his life, Ramesh asked, "So

what is it you want from life? What is it that you're looking for?" The lawyer gave it some thought and then said that he would like to be comfortable with himself and with others. This synthesizes and succinctly states what virtually every one is seeking—comfort, peace with themselves, and peace with others. Ramesh's premise is that the recognition of the functioning element, even at an intellectual level, will go a long way to bringing about this peace and harmony in day-to-day living, this comfort with oneself and with others.

When one understands it is Consciousness that acts and it is Consciousness that has designed and constructed each of us to perform as we do, it mitigates our discomfort over the inability to do all the great things one wants, as well as our frustration with others at their behavior and their inadequacies. With that understanding comes a greater degree of acceptance of ourselves and others.

If one has peace and harmony in their life but enlightenment hasn't happened, why would that matter?

It doesn't.

Why would there still be a desire for enlightenment if one has...

There usually isn't.

♋ ♋ ♋

WHAT TO DO?

Is there anything you would advise me to do?

Yes, breath!! But other than that, I don't have general suggestions for you to follow to get to a particular place.

So really, it would be to just trust the whole thing to work itself out.

I don't even suggest that. I'm not saying trust everything to work itself out any more than I'm saying do XYZ to get this result. Perhaps I'll say show up and see what happens, see what you're moved to do, see what circumstances dictate that you do next. So, if you persist in asking me what to do, I'd say, "Do the next thing." I feel very comfortable advising you to do that because you're going to do it anyway. If it works out well, I'll take none of the credit, and if it turns out badly, I'll take none of the blame.

Now it is the nature of life and living that if you come here and you have a good experience, and it has an impact on you such that your life is made better when you leave, then you will likely have a feeling of gratitude. You may well come back and be nice to me, and that will be lovely. I'd like that. If you come here and you have an experience that is terrible, where what you get from me makes you feel violated, manipulated, and otherwise tricked and deceived, you may well go away angry. You may say nasty things about me, tell people how awful I am, and I won't like that. That will feel bad. But the understanding is that both are part of the same unfolding process, and I have no more control over the outcome of that than I do of anything else. So, I come, I sit down, people show up, and we see what happens. Sometimes the results are considered to be positive and sometimes they are considered to be negative.

I know several people who were long-time devotees and very involved in this teaching, and they ended up committing suicide. An argument can be made that it was their exposure to the Teaching that was responsible for their committing suicide. In the same vein, some people who have been long-time devotees of this teaching have had this final understanding, and the suffering through those organisms ended. So, you could say that the Teaching was a wonderful thing or a terrible thing depending on the outcome in a particular case.

♋ ♋ ♋

GIFTS

If you look back over your life, you will see that the most positive, life-changing events happened unexpectedly. They were like gifts. These milestones in your life were not things you set out to do or get. They came without your planning them, without your working to get them. In fact, if you look very closely, you may realize if you truly had been in control of your life you would have short-changed yourself. You could never have constructed those blessings; you had no idea that they even existed.

Nonetheless, working to get what you think is best is part of what happens. Sometimes you get what you're working for and sometimes you don't. That's part of the process, as well. This Teaching doesn't suggest any particular kind of behavior, either sitting doing nothing or actively pursuing whatever you want.

♋ ♋ ♋

EIGHT

If all the world is a stage, where is the audience sitting?
Anon

WHAT IS CONSCIOUSNESS?

When we talk about Consciousness or Source, we talk about it as if "it" were a thing, because our language is such that there is no other way to discuss it or even conceive of it. The moment there is mental conception, the conception must be of an object. No matter how amorphous, how undefined, how infinite the object, it is still an object with those infinite, amorphous, undefined qualities.

The pointer of the Teaching is that Consciousness is not an object; rather, it is the source and the substance of everything: both the field and the object in the field. It is total.

Only an object can be perceived in its totality. Consciousness is only perceptible in its manifest form, which is this physical universe. So, if you want to know God, look around. This is it. This is God in manifest form. The pointer of this teaching is not that you have to transcend all this mundane stuff in order to reach an immaculate uncharacterized Totality, but rather that the immaculate, uncharacterized Totality has expressed itself as *this,* the manifest world .

That pointer was very significant in my spiritual journey, because as is the case with most people, this spiritual seeking for Truth is at least initially a movement *toward* something, even if that something is not defined. We're feeling pulled towards something, and often it feels like we're trying to get home, trying to get to a point of fulfillment, of completion, of connection. The search is very much one of getting *there*. So it's often a process of homing in on "it."

Now, over the years doing this you may make progress. You may find that you experience states more in keeping with what you desire: more peace, contentment, relaxation, centeredness. You can thus judge your progress toward it. Other people will give you feedback about your progress and tell you that you're getting more spiritual, that you're not that same involved person you used to be. So there is a sense of homing in on "it." And as you home in on "it," everything that is not "it" is seen as unimportant.

What happened for me was really staggering. When I met Ramesh and was exposed to this teaching, the nature of the seeking shifted. Rather than homing in on something, the seeking shifted focus and began to move outward. The same seeking energy was operating, but now the seeking was an outward movement incorporating all the facets of this universe into what was spiritual, rather than excluding *all this* to get to that spiritual "thing." *All of this* was increasingly experienced and known to be God in its incredible variety and magnificent manifest nature. Everything became miraculous. It was a very exciting shift.

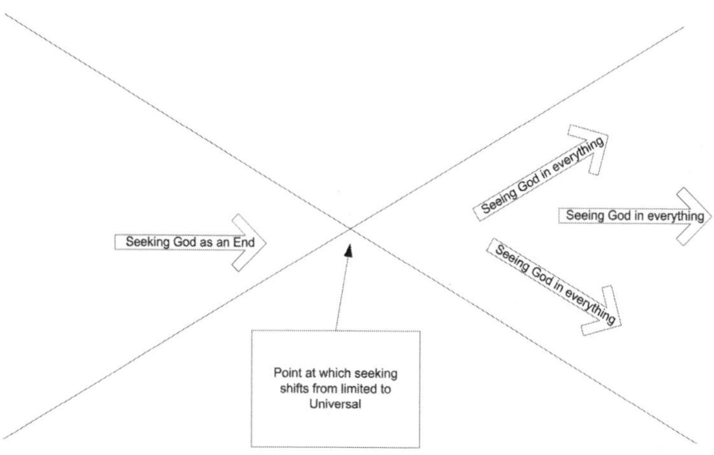

That all-encompassing movement into what is spiritual, what is true, what is "Yes!" is very life affirming; whereas, in the earlier phase of trying to get "there," so much of what is really happening is excluded. As the awareness expands to encompass everything, then everything is understood to be part of the Godliness. Even those things we don't like, the things that hurt us, the things that feel horrific—the child molesters, the torturers, the really awful things in the world—even those are accepted as aspects of That.

With this acceptance, all things are included into the spiritual presence. This is not to say that you necessarily like them. You still have the same reactions of being shocked or appalled by a particular action, but now even that reaction is included in the context of what is spiritual. It's a wonderful shift—when it happens.

WHAT DIES?

In the very simplest terms, what is born and what dies is the body/mind organism: the meat. But what ultimately is the meat? The pointer of this teaching is that everything is Consciousness; therefore, the meat is Consciousness. The mystics have often said what we truly are never is born and never dies. The Source that manifests as form—these bodies being temporary manifestations of form—never was born, nor will it die, for the simple reason that it is not an "it."

In terms of the conceptual structure of this teaching, that which fears death is called the authoring "me." It is this authoring "me" that is concerned not only with death, but also with the outcome of all kinds of things—the results—in terms of how they will affect "me;" not just as the meat, but as this authoring "me" that feels connected to the meat. "Will 'I' be able to handle it? What will become of 'me?'" Such considerations by the authoring "me" are the source not only of the fear of death, but of all suffering.

Most human organisms have a mechanistic quality of self-preservation that will act to preserve their structural integrity so that, for example, they will not put their hand into the fire or step off cliffs. We can say that the meat, while not inherently fearing death, has an aversion to it. The meat will try to preserve itself. That is very different from the fear of death, because normally what we talk about as the fear of death has to do with the fear of what will become of "me."

The strength of this authoring "me" can be, and sometimes is, considerably diminished by such things as spiritual practices and exposure to teachings such as these. Sometimes—it's certainly not automatic—the exposure to these teachings and these concepts and the presence that embodies these teachings has an effect on the authoring sense. Its reality, its validity and its potency are called into question and examined. Ultimately, that's all that really needs happen, because the authoring "me" is a chimera.

The authoring "me" is *totally* powerless. Its claims of power are utterly false. It claims authorship, but it is not the author. The authoring "me" claims whatever is happening and says, "I did that." When the results are positive, it says, "I did that well;" there's pride. When the results are negative, there's guilt over how badly "I" did it. Attendant to that there are projections into the future: "What if I don't do it well? What will happen? What will others think of me? What will I think of myself?" This is suffering, utter misery.

Ultimately, of course, even the false claim of personal authorship is not authored by this organism. We didn't create that belief in ourselves. That belief was placed in us around the age of two or two-and-a-half. You can see it happen in virtually every human being. If you observe two-year-olds, you can see the point where the child goes from operating directly in its environment as an instrument to the development of the "me." The child says, "Give ME the toy!" Before it was, "Give Billy the toy. Billy wants the toy." Now it's, "Give ME the toy!" There's a huge difference. You can feel it; you can see it happen. It is often characterized as the "terrible twos" because the whole process can be very violent and frustrating.

AUTHORING

The teaching can have its impact in a variety of ways, and the impact is on this authoring sense. If you are familiar with the teachings of Ramesh Balsekar, what he calls the doer, I call the author. When you wake up in the morning, you do all sorts of things. You go to the bathroom; you put on clothes; you think about the day ahead; you eat breakfast. The body itself dictates that these things be done: you breathe, you blink, you swallow, and you do many other things. Doing happens.

As this teaching has its effect, what is increasingly absent is a sense that "I" am authoring that doing. That sense diminishes. Obviously I'm doing it: I'm breathing; I'm washing my hair; I'm going to the bathroom; I'm making phone calls; I'm doing whatever it is I'm doing. The real thrust of what Ramesh calls the sense of doership is the sense that I am *authoring*, that I'm the *source* of the doing, as opposed to being the *instrument* of the doing. It's a distinction that may seem minor but it is crucial for realizing the nature of what is actually operative. The presumption is that "I" as this body/mind apparatus am the source for, if not everything, much of what is happening. As the Teaching has its effect, that conviction diminishes and there is more ease and comfort in daily living. You go about the actions of your day without the added stress that accompanies a strong sense of personal authorship.

♋ ♋ ♋

Events happen
Deeds are done
There is no individual doer thereof.
The Buddha

♋ ♋ ♋

VALUE

Whenever you ask if there is any value in doing something you're really asking if it's worthwhile: "Should I do it?" If you determine it doesn't have any value, then presumably you won't do it. But the pointer of the Teaching is that your role in the doing is that of an instrument. The actual question is, "Will this action have value in the future?" The only answer is, we'll have to see whether it happens, and if it happens, whether it has a desirable result. It is only in retrospect that we can sensibly talk about the value of a thing. We can say, "That's what happened. From where I stand now it appears to have been valuable." But even in saying that you're in the situation illustrated by the Chinese farmer story.

An old Chinese farmer's son leaves the gate to the corral open and his horse runs away. Now he has nothing; he's completely destitute. All of his neighbors come and say, "This is such a terrible thing. It's awful." He says, "Well, maybe." The next day the horse comes back to the corral and it's leading a band of sixteen wild horses that followed it out of the mountains. The son closes the gate, and now the farmer has seventeen horses and he's the richest man in the village. All of his neighbors come and say, "It turns out it was actually a good thing that the horse ran away." He says, "Well, maybe." The next day his son is trying to tame one of the wild horses; the horse throws him and he shatters his leg. Now he can't help the old man around the farm. Winter's coming and the old man has a real problem. All the neighbors come again and say, "Oh, it was a bad thing after all. Now you've got the horses but you don't have your son to help, and it's a terrible situation." He says, "Well, maybe." The next day the army comes through and they conscript all the able-bodied young men in the village to go fight a suicidal war, and none of these young men is ever going to come back. However, they don't take the farmer's son because he has a broken leg. So the neighbors come back . . . and the story is endless.

Where you are in the moment will determine how you judge what happened in the past—whether it was a good thing or a bad thing, whether it was valuable or not—and that perspective can shift moment to moment. Ultimately, all we can say is things happen, and we like them or dislike them in the moment based on how we perceive they affect us.

♋ ♋ ♋

What humans possess is basically
a monkey brain with a good publicist.
Colin Camerer

♋ ♋ ♋

MONKEY MIND

The chattering mind is normally thought of as the monkey mind, but it is not to be confused with the previously discussed concept of the thinking mind. The chattering mind is an aspect of the working mind. It is a process of disjointed thought activity that occurs in most brains. What makes it a problem is the involvement by the thinking mind. Whatever the working mind is doing, whether it's churning or flitting from one subject to the next, is not inherently a problem. It's simply part of what is happening. The suffering comes when there's a sense that it *shouldn't be* happening. Such secondary involvement is not present in the sage because the thinking mind is not present in the sage. Thoughts may occur, sometimes in rapid succession, sometimes in a disjointed fashion, but the real issue is always the involvement. It is the involvement by this thinking mind, by the authoring me that is the source of the suffering.

A similar analogy is that the activity of the mind is akin to monkeys chattering in the trees. If you have a tree full of monkeys outside of your window, it is likely to get quite noisy and dirty and smelly. These are aspects of the monkeys that you might not like. You may well want to see that the monkeys are removed because you don't like their effects, and there are various monkey-eradication techniques you can employ to eliminate the monkeys. The catch is that if the conditions are favorable for monkeys, they will probably return.

If you love monkeys, if your whole life were devoted to the study of monkeys, and all of a sudden monkeys move into the tree right outside of your home, the arrival of the monkeys is the greatest blessing imaginable. Now what we've really talked about here are two aspects that constitute the problem. There is the practical aspect that you as a person may well have certain inherent likes and dislikes as part of your being; you may like quiet, for example. This desire for quiet may be a component of your nature, and therefore the presence of the noise will be an irritant to the organism, and you'll want to do something to remove the irritant—very practically, very directly. So you may try and do it, and you may or may not be successful in removing the irritant by getting rid of the monkeys.

What creates suffering—and this may be a fine distinction, but it's crucial—is the sense that the monkeys should not be there, that their presence is somehow an affront to the way the universe should be. It is not simply that you don't like it, but you feel it should be other than it is—which is suffering. There is a profound difference between being uncomfortable, being in pain or not liking something, and suffering.

Having identified that, then the next point of inquiry would be to see if you have the capacity to change yourself, which you may find is sort of like standing in your boots and trying to pick yourself up by your bootstraps. You can try it. Many of the things that are suggested, particularly in the non-dualistic teachings, are precisely pointed to doing that. Sometimes, when there is grace, a kind of exhaustion occurs in which one sees through this notion of lifting oneself up by one's bootstraps. It is that seeing-through which is the essential element of these paths of inquiry: What is operative here; what is working?

And so the onion is continuously peeled.

NINE

When an ordinary man attains knowledge, he becomes a sage; when a sage attains knowledge, he becomes an ordinary man.
Zen saying

WAKING UP

My ultimate feeling about teachers and their teachings is summed up in the fact that none of them are telling the truth, so it's not a matter of reconciling one teaching with another to determine which one is the truth. None of them is the truth. When someone claims that what he or she is saying is the truth, run like hell with your hand firmly on your wallet. The truth cannot be spoken. The truth cannot be experienced in its entirety. It can only be known in its aspect.

When I hear another teacher's pointers, and they are consistent with the ones I use, I say I like it—I like that conceptual structure of pointers. What I'm saying is it appeals to my sensibility. I'm not saying he's telling the truth and some other teacher isn't. I'm saying this is consistent with how I like to see it expressed. It is aesthetically pleasing to me.

There is often a tremendous love for the teacher and the Teaching. Depending on your nature, you may personalize it as an emotional response to the teacher, or if you're more intellectual, you may love the structure of the Teaching: how it feels; its elegance and completeness;

its integrated wholeness; how it answers your fundamental questions. One can develop a tremendous love and affection for either the teacher or the Teaching, or both.

I must confess to an aversion to those teachings that suggest there is nothing you as en egoic individual can do EXCEPT allow awakening to happen. My objection is that it leaves people with tremendous guilt, because IF you have the power to awaken—by just "seeing it" or by just "being what you already are"—and you haven't done so, then you must be some kind of idiot. You are urged to look around you. Everyone else in the room is waking up (and presumably then giving similar satsang). All you have to do is "allow it to be." What could be simpler on the face of the earth than to allow what already is to be?

It seems on the surface to be a magnificent teaching, an open, loving, embracing, generous, kind teaching. But to my mind, there's an insidious kicker in there. The insidious kicker is that if you are cursed with being honest with yourself and you can see that the waking up hasn't happened, then the presumed reason it hasn't happened is because you were just too stupid, lame, or idiotic to do the most simple thing on earth.

♋ ♋ ♋

You are a puppet,
but in the hands of the infinite,
which may be your own.
Antonio Porchia

♋ ♋ ♋

DOES GOD KNOW EVERYTHING?

The very question "Does God know everything?" sets up the relationship between us as individuals and Consciousness as an object. Whether we call it Source or Consciousness or God or Totality, we are objectifying it as a sentient object. Then we talk about "it" knowing, because a sentient object can know, and we say we, as lesser sentient objects, can't know.

We really have to root out the notion that Consciousness is an object that would know something. Consciousness is not an object, nor are we separate from Consciousness. That which we point to when we use the term "Consciousness" is the totality of everything of which we are part. So, there is no '"we" and "it." We are That. We are an aspect of That, as is everything. As an aspect, we cannot possibly know the Total. We could only know the Total if we were separate from it, if we were in a subject/object relationship. Since that which is pointed to is not an object, we, as subject, cannot know it any more than you are able to lift yourself up by your bootstraps while standing in your boots. If there is no object, there is nothing to know. So we can know the Totality in aspect, we can know the Totality in some of its multitudinous parts, but we cannot know the Totality itself.

♋ ♋ ♋

NOTHING HAPPENED

Enlightenment is not the presence of the understanding that there is no one; it is the complete removal of that which could have this understanding. We talk about enlightenment as if something happens. The ultimate understanding is that *nothing* happened. Everything is as it always has been: part of an incredible tapestry of Presence.

Again, it must be repeated that these are pointers. When you ask a sage to tell you what happened, his response is always merely a pointer. But you hear it as a literal description. You hear the words and think, "Aha! I see what he means." The description brings forth an image in your mind and you can relate it to your own spiritual experience. You now know something about this. You can hook it into what you know, build upon what you know, and expand your knowledge base so you have some sense about what is being said. That's not Truth. You have expanded your knowledge base with more pointers, but the pointers are knowledge, not the Truth. The Truth is *beyond* all conceptual knowing or understanding

We give the various aspects of Consciousness labels so that we can identify them. Yes, everything is Consciousness—everything. But if we stop there there's no way for us to function because we can't know what anything is. We can't talk, we can't move around because there's no "us" to move around in any space. In the manifest world, there is both Wholeness *and* the appearance of separateness. The appearance of separateness is part of the Whole.

The organism we call the sage doesn't *know* that it is the Whole. The organism *experiences* the separateness, but it *is* the Whole. So the conflict of appearance versus the Whole doesn't exist. They both coexist.

The appearance of separateness is integral to this dance of life and living. It is the means through which all sorts of involvement happen. Yes, there's incredible suffering that arises, but there also arises amazing drama and scope in life. It exists. Why it exists, one can only speculate, but it does exist. That's the point. It is an aspect of "what is."

The conceptual tools we have for understanding and for functioning within the manifest world are not necessarily negative. The whole structure of life is built on concepts. We can say concepts are limitations, but limitations are essential for the functioning of the organism. If the organism took in everything, had to process everything without conceptual limitations, the brain would fry in a heartbeat. There's too much happening all at once for the brain to deal with. We wouldn't be able to function at all. I watch autistic kids and the way they look around at things, and it feels to me like they are overloaded. The world is just whooshing in on them. These are human organisms that don't seem to have the conceptual mechanism to limit perception, create order and make it all "sensible." Perhaps they don't function "normally" because those functional qualities of mind aren't present.

♋ ♋ ♋

AFTER ENLIGHTENMENT

After the final understanding, is there any sense of "I" in the universal sense?

Not in the way that you experience the universal "I" as a seeker. That is no longer possible because the seeker—that separate element that experiences that universality—is gone.

Once the sense of authorship disappears, is there the feeling that things are happening spontaneously and perfectly?

No. The secondary evaluation that they are happening perfectly, that they're happening spontaneously, does not arise. The sage responds directly in the moment, simply as an instrument of response, but does not experience it as such.

So does the sage still experience emotions like before?

Yes, directly and powerfully, because the organism is the instrument of the emotions. The human body/mind mechanism has an emotional component. Some are more emotional, some are more intellectual, and some are more action oriented. The balance of those elements is different in everyone. That balance describes a human organism, regardless of whether or not there is any sense of personal authorship. However, when the sense of personal authorship is gone, those elements are free to express without restriction.

♋ ♋ ♋

CHOICE

I can see that I act out of my genetic predisposition, but isn't there a part of me that chose my genetic predisposition?

Well, that's worth looking at. Can you find a part of you that chose that? If so, how is it you were smart enough to choose to be beautiful, healthy, loving, and intelligent, and somebody else was such an idiot that they chose to be deformed, ill, perverted and disgusting?

That's a judgment call that one would be better than the other. Often someone with a lower IQ might have a much more sweet and simple existence—much less complicated.

That's very true. But people who are child molesters are not having a more uncomplicated, serene, pleasant existence. They are persecuted, they are miserable; they are driven to live a horrible existence. So who "chose" to do that? That's my question. I am not here to provide the answer. It's the people who say that you choose your own destiny that don't make any sense to me.

But people do make those choices every day.

Which ones?

Well, to be child molesters—all the people that are suffering—aren't those people choosing to make those choices?

They are choosing to suffer? You think so? You're saying that child molesters, alcoholics, drug addicts are people who have chosen this miserable life?

It could be their genetic disposition to have alcoholic tendencies; you inherit that from your parents.

Right. But where's the choice in that?

That you chose your parents, you chose to be born of the loins of alcoholics, addicts.

Why would you do that?

Exactly! We're back to that question: why you would choose a miserable life?

Exactly.

But, yet, people do!

They do?

People are born into families of alcoholics or child rapists.

Yes, they are, but where is the choice part? You say, "We choose." What is the nature of this thing that chooses? That's what we keep getting back to. What are we really? And the whole thrust of this teaching is not to give you an answer, but to keep pushing you back into finding out for yourself what you truly are. What are you truly? We trace you back to genetic predisposition and subsequent conditioning. But then you very rightly say, "Okay, but where does this DNA come from?" And this is what we're doing in these talks: we're looking back to the source. I'm not going to tell you what the Source is. The work needs to be done by you.

By the Source, do you mean the Absolute, the Divine or the Self? Is that what you're going for?

I'm not going for anything.

But it's the one thing that manifests all things.

Perhaps.

Perhaps?

It's worth looking at.

♋ ♋ ♋

True knowledge exists in knowing that you know nothing.
Socrates

♋ ♋ ♋

PARTIAL AWAKENING OR SPIRITUAL EVOLUTION?

There is a prevalent notion that there can be awakening or Realization that comes and goes and finally stabilizes after some time. I do *not* believe that there is such a thing as "partial realization." I recognize there is seeking. I recognize there is intellectual understanding and there is spiritual experience, both of which are progressive and cumulative. And I recognize there is the final understanding, which is sudden, irrevocable, and after which there can be no further process, in the same way that you cannot be "more dead." You can only be dead; you can't be dead plus. Once dead, there is no question of stabilizing into your deadness. And realization, or the final understanding, is exactly like that.

In my definition of this final understanding, gradual or evolutionary enlightenment is not possible. What that refers to is this unveiling process of seeking in which you have spiritual insights. In that stage, there are often very real spiritual experiences in which you know the oneness of things. Such experiences ebb, and then they often come back again. That's what I call the process of spiritual seeking. This process has been redefined as enlightenment or awakening. In fact, much of the modern satsang movement is based on that model of spiritual experience being called enlightenment. So, after the seeker's spiritual experience has been officially declared enlightenment by someone who had their spiritual experience declared to be enlightenment by someone else who once flew over Lucknow, they are enlisted to go teach that to others as being awakening or enlightenment.

Part of the appeal of such a model is that the goal of virtually every seeker is to gain this enlightenment. Therefore, if you tell them that they gained it, they're happy because they're getting what they wanted, and they are delighted with the teacher for giving it to them. If they're honest and they say, "Well, this enlightenment, this thing that was so profound and important seems to have gone or ebbed," then the teacher says, "Well, it isn't really gone, you're just settling into it. You're just learning your new spiritual body. Your physical being is learning how to accept it" or some similar explanation often accompanied by a supporting quote from a sage who has been dead long enough to no longer be controversial. Implicit in the notion that enlightenment is progressive is that enlightenment is a state—an experiential state. The pointer in this teaching is that it is not an experiential state; an experiential state is by its nature transitory. If you're experiencing something, it will change. The very basis of duality is change. It's integral to experience. In fact, what we call life is movement and change. In the absence of this movement, when it's localized in an organism, that state is what we call death.

So in terms of the experience of life, the states of life are always alternating, but this is not what is pointed to in this teaching as enlightenment. It is why sages like Nisargadatta Maharaj would speak from the standpoint of Totality and say things like, "I'm awake even when I'm asleep. I will live even after I am dead." He was linguistically pointing to that which is not conditional. That which is the source and substance of everything—what we "truly are"—is not experiential except in its aspect. It's experiential only as what we can know and touch and taste and live. But enlightenment is beyond that kind of knowing because it is beyond the limit of experiential knowledge.

♋ ♋ ♋

SELF-INQUIRY

Asking "Who Am I?" is ultimately a ridiculous enterprise since it is clear that the mind can never know itself. But despite its very futility, the process of examining, the process of setting the mind to know itself sometimes leads to what is known in computerdom as a crash of the program. That's the value of the Zen koan or the inquiry "Who am I? What is my true nature?" What sometimes occurs is what Wei Wu Wei called "apperception," which is perception without a perceiver, knowing without a knower—non-dualistic perception. Of course, when you look into that, it is nonsense; it's meaningless. You can't possibly comprehend perception without a perceiver or knowing without a knower. The minute you know it, you know it as an object knowing something else. That's not the kind of knowing we're talking about.

So there is recognition by those of us toiling in the fields of the absurd, which is what this teaching non-duality is—truly toiling in the fields of the absurd—because what we're saying is not the truth. It is simply part of a process that is a minute aspect of "what is."

♋ ♋ ♋

TELLING A STORY

Awakening happens when the mind surrenders. The mind—and when I say the mind, I mean that aspect of the mind that believes itself the author of its thoughts, feelings, and actions—when it is destroyed, that is what we call awakening. It is a happening. This event happens, and prior to the event happening are other events, other things that happen—experiences, practices, intentions, desires.

So we tell a story about that, and say that various things that came earlier *caused* the awakening. But it's only a story. My understanding is that if this awakening is to happen as part of the functioning of the universe, then the necessary ingredients will be provided. If it is to be facilitated through surrender, then the surrender will happen. If it is to be facilitated through a guru, then the guru will appear. If it is to be facilitated through a practice, then the practice will be presented and the energy necessary to sustain that practice will also be there.

Yes, there are numerous techniques that exist within the structure of the world that *may* facilitate your getting to where you want to go. The pointer of this Advaita teaching is that the existence of those techniques, the interest on the part of someone to practice those techniques, and the effect of the technique on that person, are all connected with the destiny of that individual. While there are many techniques, none carry any guarantees and, in fact, all have widely different effects depending upon who is practicing. So, we can say that these techniques exist and they are part of the nature of "what is"—this manifest world. They will have some kind of effect, but we have no way of predicting in any particular case what will be that effect.

So the bad news is there is nothing you as an egoic individual can do to bring about this state that you want. The good news is there is nothing that you as an egoic individual can do to inhibit or stop that from happening, if it is the destiny of your body/mind organism to have such an event happen.

As a person, I certainly hope that what people experience with me is beneficial. I hope that whatever happens here has a positive impact on them. As a teacher, I am well aware that this teaching is an instrument and that I, as Wayne, am an instrument as well. Sometimes I'm an instrument for tremendous insight; other times I am an instrument for confusion.

Obviously, if I had my preference, I would be an instrument for joy, love, happiness—everything good all of the time. People are nicer to me when they are happy. The general atmosphere is better when everybody is happy. I like it. But I do not believe that I, as an author, caused this happiness or unhappiness. I may be the instrument for the happiness or unhappiness. There's gratification when I'm the instrument of happiness; there's regret when I am the instrument of unhappiness. But there is no pride when I'm the instrument of happiness, nor is there guilt when I'm the instrument of unhappiness.

What characterizes the action of a sage is the absence of a personal agenda. There's a wonderful line in a description written by Leonard Cohen many years ago (that can be found in the front of this book). He wrote that the sage is an instrument of balance, not the eliminator of chaos, either in the universe or for himself. And the line I love so much is, "For there is something arrogant and warlike in the notion of a man setting the universe in order." To believe that things *should* be different than they are is the height of arrogance; the sage does not have such a notion. What characterizes the sage is the humility implicit in the conviction that he is merely an instrument of an incredibly complex functioning that can only be called a miracle.

POINTERS

I hope to be clear on the fact that what I say is not a refutation or a rebuttal to what another teacher may say. Each of us has our own set of pointers, and they may be quite different one to the other. Often it is impossible for these contrasting pointers to be integrated. They may ultimately be pointing to the same destination, but each may point around opposite sides of the mountain, and it is not easy to walk in two directions at once. Different teachings are suited to different seekers. My sole discomfort is with teachings that claim to be the only Truth or that suggest competing teachings are wrong or dangerous. I am offended by the absence of a fundamental humility in such a stand. Every Teaching is simply a collection of conceptual pointers—nothing more.

My personal aesthetic preference is to take what is apparently manifest and start here. There exists a perception that this is a chair and this is a book and this is a building. Furthermore, there is a point of experience through which hearing, thinking, seeing and touching happen. I like to start with this common experience, withholding judgment for the moment on whether it is real or illusory.

We can argue endlessly about the reality or unreality of what is experienced. One person will say it's real; another person will say it's unreal. I am only interested in what can't be argued: there is something that is either real or unreal. This teaching points to that presence that takes numerous forms. That it exists can't be argued. The forms can be argued: whether it's red or green; whether it's male or female; whether it's true or false. All those questions can be argued endlessly, but that which IS cannot be argued. That which would argue, IS. That which claims it doesn't exist, IS. There is IS-ness. We can argue whether you exist or I exist as separate beings, but that there IS something can't be argued. The primary pointer of this teaching is that this something is all there is.

♋ ♋ ♋

REINCARNATION

The manifest universe is incarnating and reincarnating continuously. Consciousness incarnates as this and reincarnates in the next moment as that. The process is continuous and ongoing. Birth and death; construction and destruction: this is change—reincarnation—the pulse of the manifest universe.

The confusion starts when this notion of reincarnation gets intertwined with personal authorship. The authoring "me" believes it is incarnated and then is reincarnated as a separate entity. It believes itself to be separate from the Source, and out of that false sense of separation come confusion, suffering and religion.

♋ ♋ ♋

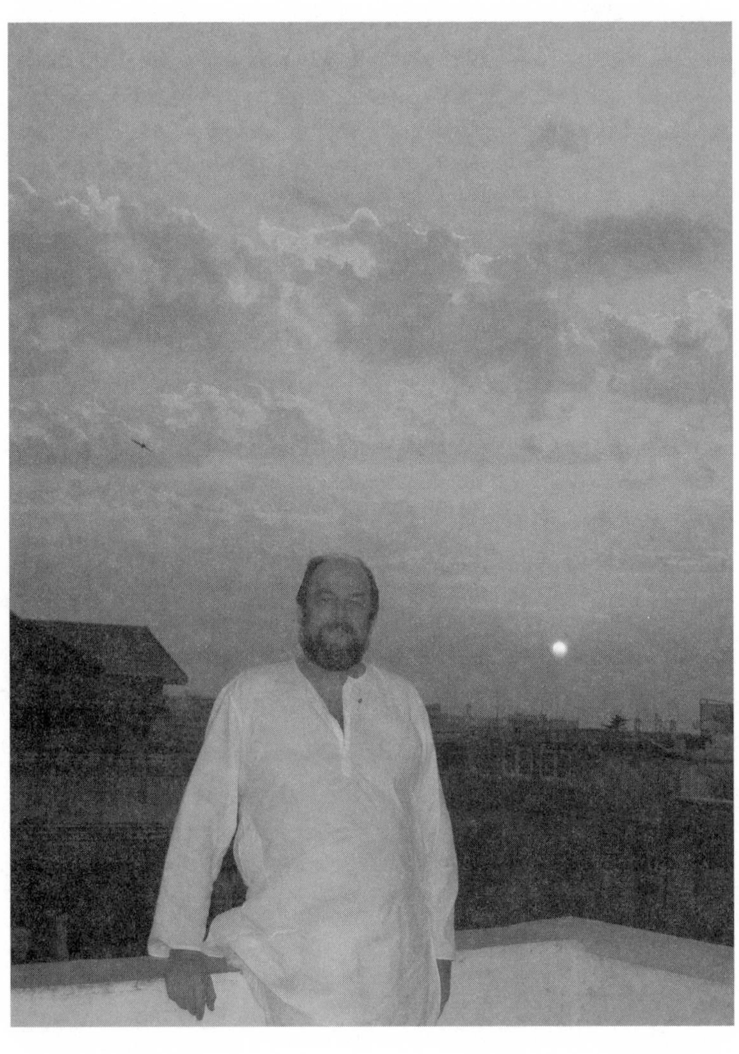

TEN

We don't see things as they are.
We see things as we are.
Anaïs Nin

INPUT: PROGRAMMING
OUTPUT: ACTION

Today, after suffering through four unrelenting hours of barking, I yelled at the dog next door. How is it that I would yell at the dog when somebody else would just sit quietly and seethe, and another person wouldn't even notice? This particular body/mind apparatus named Wayne has a certain genetic predisposition, certain intellectual capabilities, and a certain fundamental nature: it tends to be somewhat voluble. Those inherent qualities have combined with the experiences of a lifetime to compose a personality as it is today. But how is it that I yelled at the dog today after it barked for four hours when on another day I might not react at all? Well, today I received a phone call at six o-clock in the morning from somebody on the East Coast who didn't realize there's a time difference and I didn't get as much sleep as I thought I was going to, so I was a little edgy, a little irritated from having my sleep disturbed. At breakfast, my apple was wormy, and when I got down to my computer, it crashed. Those factors, completely out of my control, contributed to my reaction to the dog in that moment.

So when we look into the conditions surrounding a particular action, what we start to see is the mechanistic nature of the action itself. My yelling at the dog was the result of untold forces. What was absent in my reaction was a subsequent claim of personal authorship and involvement. "I shouldn't have done it. I should have rested serenely in my Buddha nature rather than yelling at the dog." When it is understood that the yelling at the dog happens as part of the functioning of the Universe, as part of the genetics of the organism, as part of a wide variety of circumstances outside of anyone's control, all of which combined to bring about that action, then there is peace that underlies even agitation in the organism.

There's no question that Wayne, this body/mind apparatus, was the instrument through which that yelling happened. Wayne may well be a recipient of the result of that action, as well. The neighbor may, because of his nature, take exception to my yelling at his dog and shoot me. The pointer of the Teaching is that it's all part of the same functioning. It isn't a matter of my telling my neighbor, "You shouldn't shoot me because my yelling at your dog was the functioning of Totality. It wasn't my fault." He could rightly say, "Well, shooting you isn't my fault either. It's part of the same functioning of Totality."

♋ ♋ ♋

WHO IS EXPERIENCING?

After Enlightenment, who or what is experiencing?

The organism or meat, which is an aspect of the Unity, continues to experience, but there is no *one*—a separate one—identified with it any longer.

Then there is a separate experiencer?

This is where it gets very subtle, and this is why I make the distinction between the author and the experiencer. There must remain as part of the functioning element of the organism a sense of "me." If there's no Janet associated with the organism, when this body/mind apparatus is walking down the street and somebody calls, "Janet!" it won't know to turn around. Sages, even the great ones that nobody argues about like Ramana Maharshi and Nisargadatta Maharaj—the dead ones—clearly responded when their names were called. There was identification.

Isn't it just a conditioning?

What do you mean, "*just*" conditioning? It *is* the conditioning of the organism, and that conditioning is the functioning organism called Janet. It is Janet's genetic predisposition, along with her subsequent environmental conditioning, which is the sum of all of her experiences right up to this very instant, that in total create the functioning Janet—the Janet that reacts, the Janet that thinks. Janet experiences as she experiences because of her unique programming. This organism named Wayne has red-green color confusion, so when I look out at a green tree covered with beautiful red blossoms the flowers don't pop out at me. I am unaffected by the same sight that causes others to stop and marvel at the beauty. Each organism is uniquely programmed so that it contains features common to other people and features unique to that organism. The experience of the organism is a result of the programming.

So in the body/mind organism where the sense of authorship has dropped, can conditioning continue to happen?

It can have a traumatic event, as a body/mind, and then respond to that?

Every single experience is another bit on the conditioning pile. Everything is added: everything you hear, everything you see, every moment the air touches your skin your organism is being changed. We call this change conditioning. It's a cumulative effect.

To go back to where we started this discussion, it is an absence of *horizontal involvement* with what happens in the organism that denotes this awakening or enlightenment. It is not characterized by a particular set of powers or behaviors. As such, the enlightenment is really of no particular consequence. If it were the culmination for the individual of everything that he wanted, and it provided the super-human qualities and characteristics he was seeking, then it would be wonderful from the standpoint of the seeker because he would get what he wants. But that's not it. It is the dissolution of *that which wants* to enjoy the fruits of enlightenment. It is the dissolution of that aspect of the organism that is falsely claiming these various activities that happen through the organism as "mine." That is the aspect of the organism that is the source of guilt and pride and hatred. It is that which goes when there is enlightenment.

CHANGE AND STABILITY

Life is change. So, stability, which is the absence of that change, is by its very nature temporary. There is a very human desire for stability, for constancy, for tradition. We like to have a certain repetition, so our holidays are formalized and stylized around symbols and rituals. These things are stretched throughout our life as recurring events that happen with predictability, and they have a certain flavor, a certain coloration that is familiar because of our repeated experiences with them. It is that very quality that sometimes makes them so disappointing, because sometimes they do not fulfill the promise of stability one seeks in them.

The incredible insight that Einstein brought forward was instrumental in the creation of atomic weapons that killed more people in a shorter amount of time then in any other time in history. So, clearly, there's creation and there is destruction, what we would call areas of advancement and retardation. All of that is still from a human standpoint of what is good. The fact that a lot of people were killed is only bad from the standpoint of humanity. For all the other organisms that live on dead humans—there are all kinds of bacteria, plants and such—it was an incredible bonanza! This universe is composed of those organisms, as well. They are aspects of the same creative force. There's no indication whatsoever that God favors humans over bacteria.

♋ ♋ ♋

WHY ENLIGHTENMENT?

Why do *you* want to have the ultimate understanding? What will it give you when you get it that you don't have now? Clearly, there's some sense that there is something lacking now that you believe you will have then, and so it's interesting to see what it is you're looking for. So what are you looking for?

If you are like most seekers, what you are truly seeking is happiness or peace of mind all the time. The problem is that happiness and unhappiness are two ends of the same stick. If you can find some universe that has one-ended sticks, then you can have life with just the happiness. But imagine if life were continual happiness, then there would be nothing to contrast with it and it would be dull after a while. So, unhappiness would emerge out of the happiness.

That's what the yin-yang symbol is about, the half-black, half-white symbols that fit together to form a whole. Within each side is the seed of the other: within the black side is the whole of the white; within the white is the whole of the black. You can separate it and only have the white half, but it will complete itself back into the whole—*out of itself*. It has within itself the entirety of the other—the seed of it's opposite. That's the beauty of this symbol.

♋ ♋ ♋

THE DEATH OF INSIGHT

Sometimes there is an insight that feels very fresh and clean, and then the ego takes it over and it becomes yellow and dries up. Even if one intellectually understands that it is a natural happening, there is still a feeling of loss.

You can say the reason it dried up was the ego got in there and killed it, or you can say that it had a natural life and it existed for that moment and then died as the next moment came. From the most profound perspective, what is making it happen is the functioning of life, the functioning of Totality or Consciousness—perhaps through the agency of the ego. So, yes, when the ego becomes involved, it is part of the death of that moment in terms of its impersonal freshness. But we must also understand it was *destined* to die—that its death at the hands of the ego is part of the functioning of Consciousness, part of the functioning of life, and is not *your* doing, not the result of *your* flawed perception. That, to me, is the great beauty and the tremendous freeing quality of this teaching. There may still be a feeling of loss but there is no longer any room for guilt.

♋ ♋ ♋

WHAT TO DO?

The question, "What do I need to do?" though common, is ultimately misplaced. What you need to do is whatever the next thing to do is. You need to breathe, you need to think, you need to (maybe if the impulse comes) ask a question, you need to listen; you need to do whatever the organism has been programmed to do. And it will do those things. This teaching does not suggest that you need to stop anything that you are currently doing or take on anything new. It says you will in the future do whatever it is your destiny (or nature) to do. You will do what this organism has been programmed to do in response to the environmental demands that will come. Or to put it simply: you need to live until you die.

♋ ♋ ♋

ELEVEN

The only absolute knowledge worth attaining
is that your life is meaningless. —
My life? Well now, that's another story...
Dr. Squid

THE BIG SWING

One image I find particularly useful is that this life and living is like the movement of a pendulum between polaric opposites. Early in my spiritual search, I ran across a little booklet by the Third Zen Patriarch entitled *Hsin-Hsin Ming*. In this translation it said, "The Great Way is not difficult for those who have no preferences." That really struck a chord. I saw this swinging I was experiencing was because I wanted something. I swung up towards that which I wanted, and that very energy had within it the energy to swing me back into what I didn't want. The swing always returned to the polaric opposite of what I wanted, what I was reaching for.

I had experienced through meditation and through spontaneous good fortune periods where it felt like the swinging stopped. During those periods, there was peace, centeredness, union. So, I thought, "Okay, what I need to do is to get this swinging to stop and get centered in this one-pointed presence in which there is no movement." So I began a process of ascetic practice in which I attempted to eliminate all the desires and passions that I felt would swing me in a direction toward something and ultimately swing me back into its opposite. I cut out red meat because I was told it contained the passion from the dying animal. I turned off the rock-and-roll station I normally listened to because that got me moving and pumping. I listened instead to a smooth-jazz elevator music station. That was safe. No one's passions could be stimulated by music like that! I made vague, futile attempts at suppressing my sexuality. Some things certain people just aren't suited for! I made these various efforts, and it was difficult, very difficult.

Fortunately, before I developed a permanent twitch, I met Ramesh. I explained to Ramesh what I was doing, how I was trying to stop this swinging, and he said, "Wayne, the stopping of the pendulum is better known as death." The cessation of the swing is death. Life *is* the movement between polaric opposites. He helped me understand that when the Third Zen Patriarch said, "The Great Way is not difficult for those who hold no preferences" he was talking about the *involvement* in the movement. In fact the same translator of the little *Hsin-Hsin Ming* book did a retranslation some thirty years later and in his new translation he changed the line from "The Great Way is not difficult for those who have no preferences." to "The Great Way is not difficult for those not attached to preferences." Huge difference, you see.

Preferences are a function of the body. If there is a body and a personality connected to that body, then preferences will happen. It will like certain things and dislike others according to the conditioning of the organism. Now, the Teaching simply points to "what is." It does not tell you that you should or should not be involved in your preferences. It merely points to the obvious. That's why being an Advaita teacher is really quite simple. All I'm doing is pointing to what's here now so that your attention is drawn back to "what is." What we're describing with this pendulum model is total identification with what

I call the author. When there is identification as the author, one is identified at the very bottom of the pendulum. So when there is a swing into what is liked, there is a total swing by "you" into what is liked. When it swings back, there is a total swing into what is not liked. "You" go through big dramatic shifts.

What happens through organisms we call seekers is a process of disidentification whereby there is a movement up the pendulum shaft. As one ascends the pendulum shaft, there's less identification as the author. The swinging continues, but toward the top of the shaft, the subjective arc, the subjective experience of movement through the same event, is much less. There is a sense of being less involved with those events as an authoring "me." Occasionally one may experience moments at the very top of the pendulum shaft. During those moments, life goes on, but there is no sense of being moved by it.

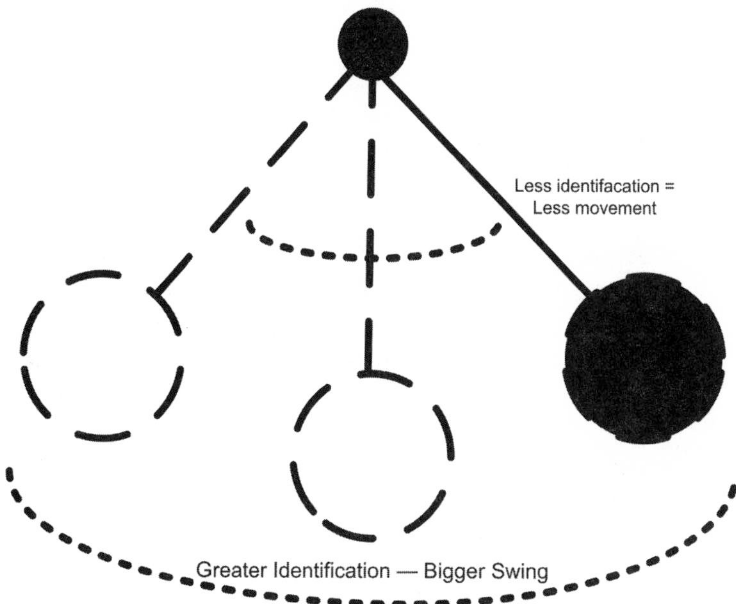

However, the inescapable fact is that it is a greased pendulum shaft. So, as you well know, something happens and there is a slide back into involvement by this authoring "me." It gets stronger and more involved, then it gets weaker, and then it gets stronger. That's the experience of the seeker. You've probably encountered teachers and teachings that say this state at the top of the pendulum—this experience of unity and oneness.—*is* enlightenment, and the sliding back into involvement, which is inevitable, is "stabilizing into your enlightenment" or "deepening into your enlightenment." Here, in this Advaita teaching, that movement in and out of involvement is simply a description of the seeking process.

This teaching is not designed to bring about enlightenment for the seeker, which helps explain why there are so few people interested in the Teaching. When people realize what's actually happening in this teaching, they realize that the Teaching is not offering a method for them to get what they think they want and need.

What they may "get" as seekers is the *experience* of more and more detachment, which is a wonderful thing for as long as it lasts. However, it *will* end! It *will* shift. Some traumatic event will happen that will precipitate a slide down into involvement. Then they're doubly screwed, because not only are they dealing with whatever they're involved in that hurts, but there's a lingering sense that they've fallen from grace. They've come down from a lofty state of unity in which there was understanding and everything was connected, and now they're back doing the big swing again.

There are some dramatic stories about this process of being at the top of the pendulum for a while and then sliding to the bottom. St. John-of-the-Cross is a classic example. He described being at the top of the shaft as "walking hand in hand with God," and then when he slid he felt *abandoned* by God. The experience was felt as a betrayal, of being forsaken. It was terrible for him; he was incapacitated. His brothers had to feed him and sustain him because he was so distraught, and for a couple of years there was absolute despair.

The depths and natures of spiritual experiences vary from ones where one touches bottom and then bounces immediately up, to others where this period lasts longer. This is a *very common* and integral part of the experience of the seeker. It is reported by most people involved in this process. The fantasy of the seeker is that enlightenment means staying at the top of the pendulum all the time. However, since there is no fixedness in the dualistic state, that is impossible. Getting to and staying at the top of the pendulum shaft is not what the sages have pointed to as awakening. Awakening is the complete dissolution of *that* which travels up and down the shaft—*that* which is identified.

Of course, you don't have any control over the process! If you did, you would stay at the top of the pendulum all of the time. But you can't do it; obviously, you can't do it. If you could, you would. So the fact that you don't points to the fact that there is some limitation in your capacity to make things happen, and that's a good place to start in terms of looking at what is the power of this authoring me. The sense that "I" can make it happen despite all evidence to the contrary is what Ramesh calls the divine hypnosis.

For the seeker there often are experiences of the authorship weakening and strengthening. Over time, there may well be appreciable progress such that there is progressively less overall involvement as the author. The teaching has its own effect. When that which strengthens and diminishes is completely dead, this is what we call enlightenment. There is often an experience attached to the moment of its obliteration. One can point to that moment, but afterwards there's no experiential reference to "that which never was."

The sage's experience of enlightenment is like your experience today of walking around without a stone in your shoe. You know what it feels like to walk around with a stone in your shoe; it's not fun. But today you have been walking around all day without a stone in your shoe. Your experience of that—of the absence of the stone—is identical to the sage's experience of the absence of the author, meaning there is none. One does not experience the absence of something. You experience something leaving, you experience the transition, and you experience the presence of something. However, you do not experience the absence of something. In the most profound sense, there is *nothing* to experience.

INSTRUMENT OR AUTHOR?

The whole point of this teaching is that it has no "supposed to," either implied or expressed, as to what you are to do or not do. The understanding is underneath the doing; it is the bedrock upon which all the doing happens. What you do is a product of your programming. And you can see this very clearly if you examine your behavior. Don't take my word for it. Examine your behavior. Look for yourself and see what fuels your actions.

You may say, "I don't know what I'm supposed to do." Fair enough. But that statement presumes you are the author of your actions, because if you are not the author then the question "What am I supposed to do?" doesn't have any meaning. It only has meaning if you're the author. If you're the instrument of the doing, then the only question is, "What will I do next?" That's the difference between being an instrument and being the author.

♋ ♋ ♋

I am not sure that I exist, actually. I am all the writers that I have read, all the people that I have met, all the women that I have loved, all the cities that I have visited, all my ancestors...

Jorge Luis Borges

♋ ♋ ♋

REACTIVITY

The ability to lessen one's reactivity in emotional responses is often considered a sign of spiritual development. But in my mind, non-reactivity usually is a sign of deadening to life. We are reactive mechanisms. In the moment, the reaction of the organism is what defines it. Through spiritual practices and various other methodologies, you can neutralize your activity and responsiveness. You can sit in meditation; you can quiet yourself; you can still your thoughts; you can still your actions. You can do that with meditation or you can do it in the way I did it for so many years: with Scotch, marijuana and rum.

To me, action and reaction represent the fullness of life. The hallmark of the sage is a total—*total*—reactivity moment by moment, not tempered in any way by secondary involvement. The damping of reaction and the damping of thoughts is a secondary involvement. The idea that one *should* act or react in a certain way is the source of suffering.

There is no particular style of reaction that characterizes the sage. A sage may react passionately and vociferously, as was often the case for Nisargadatta Maharaj, or he may act moderately and gently, as was usually the case with Ramana Maharshi.

Much of the confusion on this matter stems from what I consider to be a misinterpretation of a basic Hindu tenet: namely that the *vasanas* (the tendencies that comprise the personality) disappear as one becomes more spiritually adept. The third Chinese Zen patriarch made a similar statement observing that the sage is without preference. So, you read these texts and you think by being more neutral, by having no apparent preference, you will hasten your spiritual development. But this is not what was being suggested by the original Masters.

The preference is a function of the organism's genetic programming and all its subsequent conditioning, which combined provide a certain reaction. It may be a passive reaction or a very volatile and active one, but in neither case is it representative of spiritual condition.

The lack of *involvement* in the reactivity is indicative of lack of involvement by a "me." As the "me"—the egoic authoring sense—weakens, there is a lessening of involvement in what happens. Yet, there is total *participation* by the organism in what is happening, because it is the involvement by the "me" that mitigates or veils this participation.

♋ ♋ ♋

FEAR

Wayne, I have a question about fear. Where does it come from, and how could it occur in a personal "me" if there is only one life force—God—running everything?

There is only one life force, but it expresses itself through various instruments. These instruments are tuned to make various sounds. One of them is fear.

Yet, when I am aware of that force of life, I have no fear.

Yes. What you describe as "awareness of the life force" is synonymous with the dimunition of the authoring "me."

I have always had "regular fear," but this is something different.

Yes, it is the fear of letting go, the fear of being cast adrift in a Present in which you cannot survive.

I thought I was not afraid anymore. I try to tell myself that I can survive anything. Then, in this fear, I know for certain that I can't and I become terrified.

It is the death throes of the ego.

Then let the damned thing die already. This is awful.

I am sorry for your pain. I can only promise you that it is all unfolding perfectly?

♋ ♋ ♋

THE MECHANICS OF SPIRITUAL EXPERIENCE

Several years ago, there was a very interesting study in the field of brain research in which researchers found what was essentially the "God spot" in the brain: a portion of the brain that became active during the experience of unity. Meditation, drugs and various practices could stimulate it. When that part of the brain was active, the person reported the kind of mystical experience every spiritual seeker has felt at least once and seeks to repeat. The study confirmed what the Teaching has long pointed to, namely the experience of unity by the seeker is a relative experience and is the conditioned opposite of the experience of separation. They are alternating experiential states that occur within a body/mind organism.

What the Teaching calls the ultimate understanding or awakening is transcendent of the experiential. The sage does not have the experience of oneness, which is a transient physical state, but rather IS the Oneness. The understanding of the sage is transcendent of the organism.

♋ ♋ ♋

SUDDEN OR GRADUAL

Is the awakening gradual or is it sudden, spontaneous, and permanent?

It is gradual in the sense that your progress to the edge of the cliff is gradual. There may be five steps or five thousand steps taken before you reach the edge, but the last step is always sudden and irrevocable.

How do you take it?

"You" don't. "You" never take the step. It takes you. The ego will not willingly go over, even though it says, "I want to be free of the burden of myself." It doesn't really want to be free of the burden of itself, it simply wants to be free of its limitations and those aspects of itself it doesn't like.

♋ ♋ ♋

CONTROL

For the human organism we call the sage, the desire for control is purely functional, it is purely a matter of the operation of the organism. He wants to learn how to do things; he wants to learn the pattern of things in order to be better able to function in his environment. He is thus like every other human being.

The involved individual wants control, not only for functional reasons, but also to have the feeling of egoic strength and security. There is the idea, "If I can gain more control I will be more complete. The more I can control, the safer I will be." That's the carrot the ego holds in front of itself: "If I can get more control, this feeling of insecurity, this feeling of helplessness that stirs in me and makes me more uncomfortable will disappear." There is a sense that by gaining more power one can overcome the underlying feeling of impotence. So there is a seeking for economic, social, physical or political power, and then after it is gotten comes the realization that it doesn't help. So one turns to spiritual power, or occult power, or some other kind of power to hopefully fill that void. For the sage, there is no void, so there is nothing that needs to be filled. That desire for control is not sought as a means of gaining completion or fulfillment because that is not necessary. His is a purely functional control.

For the seeker, when the thought arises of not being in control, there is often a feeling of helplessness and a sense that without control there is nothing. So, even though there may be an intellectual conviction that it is the Source that is in control, still there is a feeling of disquiet or perhaps despair.

My observation, and you may discover this for yourself, is that the disquiet is not really about true powerlessness; it is about not having *enough* power. As long as there is the possibility of power and control, and you don't *have* it, then a feeling of disquiet or helplessness is almost inevitable.

In the *total* surrender, in the complete acceptance of one's own inherent powerlessness as an author, there is total freedom. There is a complete absence of that disquiet, and it is exactly that freedom the sages have been pointing at for millennia, giving it various names such as *ananda* or bliss. These are terms pointing to the absence of this disquiet, the absence of this suffering.

Even the person at the very top of the human hierarchy is limited and knows in some deep, central part of himself that he's susceptible, that he is not able to control, that he is of limited power. Even the president of the United States, even Bill Gates knows that he's going to die and he can't stop it, no matter what he does. That's why the sage is truly free, because he is no longer identified as the *one* who is limited; thus, he will never die . . . because what he truly is was never born.

♋ ♋ ♋

TWELVE

The mind of man may be compared to a musical instrument with a certain range of notes, beyond which in both directions we have an infinitude of silence.

John Tyndall

KNOWING ONENESS

There is nothing to become. We are all already That. We're all Consciousness. That's what everyone is: the One. There's nothing more or less than the One. But for the purposes of our discussion, we point to the fact that in most human beings there is the presence of this experience of separation as an authoring "me." In others, that sense of separation is not present. When the sense of separation was present and now is permanently no longer present, we give that event a name. Then seekers mystify the hell out of it because the Holy Grail for the seeker is to have that event happen. Yet, for the one for whom that has happened, it's of no consequence. It's simply another event in the history of the organism.

The sage is not walking around in that state of exquisite presence that the seeker experiences as an alternating state of presence and involvement. Those alternating states define each other. So the experience of presence is the experience of the seeker. Since that state is not alternating, the sage has no experience of oneness.

The sage *is* the Oneness. There can only be an experience of something when there is separation from it.

♋ ♋ ♋

PROBLEMS

One approach to understanding your true nature is to delve deeply into your problems. If you go deeply enough, you can see, conceptually at least, that there is no substance to them. You probably won't feel the same attraction to deconstruct the blessings; you will just enjoy them. There's much more energy available for looking into your pain or your discomfort because there's a desire to get out of it. The mind says, "If I can understand it, maybe I can make it go away."

You'll realize as you investigate your unhappiness, there is no substance to it; yet, prior to the investigation, it's very much a part of your reality. So we can start with the fact that unhappiness is an aspect of this manifest world. We can go underneath it and with insight see that it has no independent existence, but there is a point of substance even in that inquiry, and the point of substance is that which is looking. That which is examining the illusion is itself substantive. It must be.

The inherent problem that you will undoubtedly run into, as does everyone in whom this examination takes place, is where do you stand to gain perspective on that which is looking? How can the eye see itself except in reflection? It can see an image in the mirror, but that which it sees is only an image. The eye cannot see itself, and that which is investigating cannot see itself since it is not separate.

So, the purpose of inquiry is to point one back to That which is looking. That which is looking is elemental. It is in fact Consciousness. This that you believe yourself to be is an instrument through which the looking happens. New instruments through which perception happens are being created all the time. They are being recycled at a phenomenal rate. Not only human objects, but all objects with senses are points of perception through which Consciousness functions.

When you inquire honestly and deeply you will get to a place of not knowing. And it is precisely in the not knowing that insight comes. Once you know something, then it's shelved and it's dead. This is not to denigrate knowledge. Knowledge can be very useful in the moment. The intellect can also be the instrument through which insight comes in the moment. But when the ego takes this knowledge and claims it as its own, this knowledge becomes a burden.

Here's an example: As a seeker, you're going along your path and you come to a river too deep and fast to cross. What you find is that some generous guru has left a beautiful conceptual boat on the shore for you. You are free to hop in it and cross the river. Once across, you are so impressed with this vehicle—how wonderful and how useful it is and how fortuitous it was to come into your life at exactly the right time—that you pick the boat up, throw it on your back and carry it with you. Now it is a burden; it actually slows you down. What was once a facilitator becomes a hindrance to your progress.

It doesn't matter where these pointers come from; in the moment their usefulness can be profound, but as soon as they are claimed by the ego, they become a burden. So it is in that state of non–involvement that you're traveling freely and lightly.

♋ ♋ ♋

CONTROLLING THOUGHTS

There are numerous thought control techniques. Some of them may work at certain times but not at others. Some may work for certain people but not for others. But if you look at any technique, what you'll notice is that the impulse to employ the technique is a thought. You can't control the thought that prompts this controlling energy. You may find a technique that works well for you, and yet you may find you don't employ it all the time. Why is that? How is it that even when you are avidly applying your technique, sometimes there are random, vagabond thoughts that slip through the screen?

The ego crows, "I have made my thoughts stop by employing this technique." But upon deeper investigation, it may be seen that it was Consciousness that made the thoughts stop through your application of the technique. The thought arose to learn the technique in the first place. The energy was provided within you to keep going back and perfect the technique. And then the thought arises from time to time to employ the technique. All of which, if you look at it, isn't authored by you. You're doing it, obviously; the thought is occurring in your mind. But are you the source for the thought? That's the question that this teaching asks. Who or what is the source? Is it you? Or is it something bigger than you of which you are a part?

ILLUSION

The concept that all that is manifest is an illusion is a teaching tool that has been used for millennia, and despite its longevity, it is often misunderstood. What is illusory is that everything *appears* discrete and independent, when in fact all are aspects of the same Unity, even though the connection is not readily visible. What is apparent is that everything is separate. So we talk about and operate on that basis of the appearance, when in fact everything is an aspect of Consciousness. That's the importance of the concept of illusion. It is sometimes mistakenly believed that when there is the awakening then all that is manifest is seen through as false or somehow disappears.

When the sage cuts himself and there's blood spurting out, he has cause for concern. There's sufficient identification with the body/mind mechanism that he seeks help. He doesn't say, "Well, that's just a lousy illusion that I'm bleeding to death. It's a good thing I know this isn't real." The human organism functions as a human being. This is why I make the distinction regarding the sense of separate authorship. Separate authorship is that sense that this organism is not only an independent object, but that it also is the author of its activities. In truth, humans are the instrument *through which* incredible forces of the universe operate to produce evolution, love, culture, knowledge, etc. The source of the suffering is specifically this quality in which the organism usurps the subjectivity of God. But it is absolutely crucial to remember that *it was NOT the organism that decided of its own volition to do that.*

What I've been pointing to all along is that the volition claimed by the "me" is an illusion, so it can't possibly be the organism that created it. That's where this teaching diverges from many so-called Advaita teachings, because they say that to Wake Up is the one decision that the individual can make, while the individual has no volition over anything else. The way I understand such a concept is that there is only one thing left for you to screw up: Waking Up. If you have the power to simply allow the waking up to happen and you don't do it, then you must be the biggest idiot of all time! Of course, it is more desirable for the ego to think of itself as an idiot than to think of itself as impotent.

The emphasis of this teaching is that *even the illusion of separateness as the author is the functioning of Totality*; this divine hypnosis is part of the functioning of Totality. Ramesh called it divine hypnosis, because it's not *self*-hypnosis. It's not that at age two-and-a-half you hypnotized yourself into believing that you were separate. It is part of the nature of things as they are now that virtually every human has this illusion of separateness.

The illusion of separateness occurs in the same way that your nose occurs on your face: you didn't put it there. You don't have any capacity to put a nose on your face, yet, there it is. In you is the sense of personal authorship. You can say it's nonsense. You can say I don't want it. You can say all sorts of things about it, but it's there in the same way that the nose is on your face. It's there.

So if you didn't put it there, then it must be part of a greater functioning, the product of influences far bigger than your egoic self. That is the pointer of the Teaching: the presence of the ego, as well as the presence of everything else, is part of the functioning of Totality.

♋ ♋ ♋

FATALISM?

In what you just said, and in Acceptance of What Is, *I hear an undercurrent that reincarnation may be bullshit. In essence, the bodies are basically these balloons for experience. And the idea, the comforting thought of reincarnation or Christian life after death is bullshit . . . I'm hearing the possibility that what happens when you die is that you're just absorbed back in Oneness, and that the experience through that separate balloon that popped out for a little while, ends.*

Very close. The pointer isn't that you are reabsorbed into Oneness, but *you were never separate from Oneness;* therefore, as an aspect of that Oneness, that particular aspect ceases to be. The Oneness remains.

And for me, as this human balloon, the feeling is fatalistic. "Okay. Who gives a shit?" Maybe the way I've been operating my life is quite fine; just ignore it and keep going until I die. There is nothing to think about, nothing to worry about, nothing to obsess about. It just happens and that's it. Am I close?

And who cares?

Right.

This is really the question: Who cares? And it's not a fatalistic question; it's actually a very deep and profound question.

♋ ♋ ♋

We must dare to think about "unthinkable things"
because when things become "unthinkable"
thinking stops and action becomes mindless.
William Fullbright

♋ ♋ ♋

I AM THAT

I Am That is a book I've been unable to read. I've picked it up half a dozen times over the last fifteen years or so because it's an important book in the history of this teaching, but there's no point of connection for me in that book.

It's significant that books are like that. People come to books in the same way that they come to teachers or teachings, and they are sometimes incredibly moved by them. That was my experience with Ramesh. I was deeply moved by his presence and what happened in the space around him. When I tried to bring my friends to his talks, those that came felt that he was a very nice Indian man with some interesting things to say, but they were unmoved to return, whereas I could not stay away. The pull was very powerful to be there.

In order to explain this phenomenon I came up with a concept called "resonance." The structure of this concept is that resonance occurs between two objects. Body/mind mechanisms are objects, each with unique qualities and characteristics. If there is resonance between the seeker object and the guru object, then out of that resonance there arises an experience of the Guru, with a capital G. The guru object (with a small "g") can be a person, a mountain, a book or a picture. So when there is this resonance, then the Guru is made manifest for the seeker object.

In the absence of that resonance, there is no experience of the Guru. This explains how people can be in the same space with a particular teacher, or people can be driving their car past a particular mountain, and some will feel incredibly moved by the event and others won't even notice it. It is out of the resonance that this experience is born. So, with *I Am That* I have no resonance. Yet, the Teaching that came through Nisargadatta to Ramesh, and through Ramesh to me, is one that I value very highly.

♋ ♋ ♋

DECISIONS

There are five frogs sitting on a log. Three of them decide to jump off. How many are left?

No, not two. There are five left. The mere fact that they've decided to jump off does not mean that they have jumped. We decide all kinds of things. Whether or not that decision translates into action, we can't predict.

You need only look at your own experience. If the results of your decisions were in your control then all your decisions would result in the decided action. But I have yet to meet anyone who can tell me honestly that all of their decisions resulted in subsequent action.

If you look more deeply into it, you will see that this is actually a good thing. If you select the three most profound events that happened in your life and ask yourself if they were a result of your plan or your decision, almost without fail people report that the most significant events in their life came unexpectedly. What happened could not have been planned because they didn't even know it existed. They didn't know that the person they fell in love with was on the planet. They didn't know that a wonderful teaching existed, yet it fell into their lap.

In my case I wasn't looking for a guru or for some arcane Hindu philosophy to come into my life, yet, I would count that as one of the greatest blessings in my life. If I had been the architect of my life, I couldn't have built that. I didn't know it existed.

So the fact that we are not the architects of our destiny is in fact a tremendous blessing, not the horrible state the ego will say it is.

♋ ♋ ♋

JUST HAPPENING

If I understand this Teaching correctly, whatever is there is there for me, and it's just a matter of me moving into that. I will be led through a thought or feeling to do an action that will lead to something else. I sort of understand that intellectually, but I don't know how it works in day-to-day living.

The Teaching simply describes what happens. It is not a blueprint for telling you what you should or shouldn't do; it is a descriptor. It points to the fact that in the moment you will react to a stimulus in accordance with your unique programming. What that reaction will be, you have no way of knowing. You can only describe what happened after the fact. "I got the past due notice. I realized they were going to cut off my electricity, and that prompted me to go get a job." So you act in accordance with your nature.

Not judging if it's right.

Your nature may be to judge it right or wrong. Even the judgment is happening in accordance with your nature.

And that's just part of all that is.

I would agree with you, except I would take out the "just." It is *all* part of what is, not *just* part of what is. It is all part of what is, because that is what is happening. The uncertainty is part of what is happening; the doubt and the fear are all part of what is happening in the moment when they arise. Even the "should" that arises as a function of having a sense of personal authorship is understood to be part of the same functioning, not some misguided action on your part.

It just is.

It IS, not "just is." It IS. What you're saying (and I hear it said in virtually every talk) is, "If I'm not doing it, it's *just* happening. When I do it, it has real substance. When it's happening, it's *just* happening." That is the blustering of the ego, claiming primacy. It's a macho, chest-beating kind of action on the part of the ego. The ego has no substance. It has no power. It can do nothing except claim primacy. The problem from the standpoint of the ego is that the evidence abounds that it is impotent—totally impotent—because if it were truly in control your life would look a lot better; it would do everything in its power to make you the center of everything. You'd be successful and powerful and kind and generous and loving and everything good, all the time—perfectly. But it's not powerful, and thus, you are as you are.

There is a wonderful story about a rabbi who goes into the sanctuary. He sees the Torah sitting in the Ark, and he's so overwhelmed with the truth and beauty and completeness of it that he falls to his knees in front of the Ark and cries, "God, I am nothing! I am nothing!" The associate rabbi is walking by the sanctuary and looks in and sees this incredible display of piety by the head rabbi. He's so taken that he can't help himself, and he rushes down to the front of the sanctuary and falls to his knees next to the chief rabbi and cries, "God, I am nothing! I am nothing!" (In Jewish temples there is always a non-Jew who is hired to work around the Temple, because on the Sabbath Jews can't do any work. Theoretically, they are not even supposed to turn on lights. So a non-Jew has to do all the work, and this person is called a *shamas*.) So, the *shamas* is walking by the sanctuary and he sees the two rabbis there. He is so moved by their incredible display of piety that he rushes down to the front of the sanctuary, falls to his knees next to the rabbis, and beats on his chest crying, "God, I am nothing! I am nothing!" The first rabbi nudges the second rabbi and says, "So, look who thinks he's nothing!"

PRESENCE AND ABSENCE

There is a great difference in having the belief that you are not the author and not having the belief that you are the author.

It is not a semantic difference, though I use semantics as a pointer to the difference. The *presence* of the belief that I'm not the author is an intellectual understanding that is relative. In the *absence* of the belief that I am the author, there is no belief involved at all; there is only the absence. There is not the presence of the belief I am not the author.

The intellectual understanding that you're not the author is a relative understanding. It is going to come and go, as do all things in relativity. The only immovable spot is the absence of this dualistic movement, the absence of both. It is why this is sometimes called "the negative way," or the way of emptiness or absence, because it isn't the *presence* of knowledge or an understanding about the way things are, but rather the *absence* of conviction and knowledge about the way things are.

THIRTEEN

I am what I am.
Popeye

ROOTS

Advaita and Taoism have their roots in the same pool, as do all the major spiritual traditions. Those two—Taoism in particular—may be the ones that have maintained their non-dualistic essence much more than any of the others. Interestingly, a viable religion never formed around Taoism. There was a period during which a kind of mystical sex cult formed, and that lasted for a few hundred years, but it didn't survive. There was no bureaucracy of priests or monks who were in the business of sustaining an organized structure.

Both have at their root this essential teaching of "everything is One." This basic teaching was often misunderstood and misinterpreted by people who didn't have the complete understanding. However, when they had positions of authority and respect within their social structures, their words and their teachings became enshrined. Inevitably, in the history of all religions such things happened.

Ramana Maharshi, Ramesh Balsekar and Nisargadatta Maharaj are the more famous contemporary voices that talk about what I would call pure Advaita. Advaita Vedanta on the other hand is a religion with an entrenched swami class, with rules and rituals that, to my mind, are completely superfluous to the essential teaching.

What intrigued me upon meeting Ramesh was that I felt in his presence there was Truth. It wasn't in the conceptual framework, but I knew the Truth was there. There was a resonance that produced an experience of connection. Then as I began to understand this teaching, I was completely captivated by it, because it was so basic and pure in its pointing.

Even though the Teaching itself is quite austere and unornamented, there exists within it the potential for tremendous passion. The notion that everything that exists is an aspect of God is actually a very passionate, sexy teaching. It's saying that the flowers, the juices in your body, the urges in your being, the excitement, the fear, the life, the death, and all these qualities that exist are aspects of the incredible presence of God.

♋ ♋ ♋

THE SOLDIER AND ADVAITA

There was an incredibly poignant moment during Ramesh's retreat in Germany several years ago. He was talking about one's mechanistic nature and that one never knows what one will do in any given situation. One may say, "I have moral standards. I have convictions. I would behave this way. I would never do that." But one never really knows what one will do until the moment comes.

An older man came forward and said, "What you just said struck me very deeply. During World War II, I was a German soldier and we were sent to France. The partisans ambushed us and killed a number of my friends. My best friend died in my arms. After that, I went into that village and killed innocent women and children in cold blood. I would have never imagined that I was capable of such a barbaric act, and I've lived with the guilt of that for my entire life, until coming to this teaching. I have come to understand that those actions—the actions of the partisans, my actions, the actions of all those around me—were part of an enormous functioning, a part of "what is." It could not have been otherwise." He had tears in his eyes and his voice was choked with gratitude. He had seen clearly that he had played out his role and in the seeing had been relieved of a crushing burden.

The blessing of the Teaching is the freedom that comes with the understanding that it could not have been otherwise. The freedom comes in the recognition that one's acts, however horrible, are part of an unimaginably huge and complex functioning. Tomorrow, that man might be arrested and tried for what he did sixty years earlier, but that would be an externally imposed sanction. The teaching eased the guilt that he had to live with for so many years. Through the impact of the Teaching he was able to see that we function as part of a much bigger process, and in the seeing of that, there was peace—a peace that the Bible talks about as "the peace that surpasses all understanding." It is a peace that coexists with whatever is, regardless of how beautiful or how ugly.

BEYOND ENLIGHTENMENT

In the most profound sense, when enlightenment happens, the whole notion of enlightenment becomes moot because there isn't any one to know he's enlightened. There isn't any actual thing as enlightenment, because the ultimate understanding is that every thing Is. All is an incredible oneness made manifest in this life and living. That's the understanding. Words inevitably fail, because what they point to is not experiential. Therefore, enlightenment is not a knowing in the way we know that the chair is black. That is a subject/object knowing. The ultimate understanding is a knowing that is without a knower. It is the knowing that is intrinsic, that is fundamental and independent of experience.

♋ ♋ ♋

WHO CARES?

I keep going around in circles. There must be something that transcends the circles. I don't want to be a seeker for that, but conceptually I grasp that there is something that is transcending the circles.

You've been around the spiritual block enough so that you know that you really don't want to be a seeker because being a seeker is a limiter. The "spiritually advanced" Advaita understanding is that seeking is ultimately an obstacle. And so, you've got a whole upper echelon of seekers who are wandering from satsang to satsang saying, "I'm no longer a seeker."

I'm here. I came to see you, so I must be a seeker or something.

"Or something." We can give it another name if being a seeker has a bad name. We can call it something like "you're someone that enjoys being in the presence." But I have no problem with the notion of a seeker. Yes, the seeking is ultimately an obstruction, but it is the *seeker* that is dissolved in the final understanding, and with its dissoulution is the dissolution of the seeking.

Furthermore, the spiritual seeking can stop prior to this understanding happening, and it certainly does in many cases where people move on and get a life and do other things—take up bridge or mountain climbing or stamp collecting or knitting.

Who is doing it?

The same "who" that wants to know who is doing it; the same "who" that asked the question, "Who is doing it?" is doing it. That organism—that body/mind mechanism born to your parents, educated in the schools you went to, all of that combination of genetic material, plus experiences—does things. Now we can make esoteric statements about how it's all an illusion and no one is doing anything and nothing is happening and you don't exist; that's fine. But for the moment, a question appeared. It appeared through an organism. We have a shared experience of that. We can use that as a starting point.

What fuels all this activity: the asking of the questions, the thoughts, the hearing of the questions, the response? Is there something common to all of that activity? The pointer of this teaching is back to the Source of all activity.

Everywhere.

Everywhere—whether it's the subatomic activity of electrons and waves and particles, or the macro activity of the cosmos. Is there something common to all of it? The teaching pushes you to expand the focus from this narrow band of conceptualizing you generally have, to looking at things from a bigger perspective.

Ramana was pointing back to the Source with this question, "Who am I?" Start there. Start with what you've got. You've got this. Okay, what is this? Look into that which is asking the question so the attention is turned back on itself. You've got the Advaita 101 answer, "What I truly am is Consciousness." Now that you have that answer, you have to discard it and look deeper.

I don't know.

"I don't know" is an excellent place to start. It opens the door to a deeper understanding.

♋ ♋ ♋

Beyond the pairs of opposites
of which the world consists,
other, new insights begin.
Herman Hesse

♋ ♋ ♋

NEVER MIND

If one wants to remain in that moment, what does one do about the mind?

That's why I say, "Never mind!" The mind does what the mind does. It is working and functioning perfectly, doing exactly what it has been designed and programmed to do, including *everything* it does. So where is the question of controlling it or directing it? Who wants to do that?

The separated sense of self . . . that is part of the mind . . . that is the mind.

So the Teaching invites an investigation of who wants to control the mind. What is ultimately the source of that desire to control the mind?

What is the source of that which wants to control the mind? I don't know.

That's an excellent place to start.

♋ ♋ ♋

PHYSICAL PAIN

Different organisms have vastly different capacities for enduring physical pain. I know people who can't endure the pain of having their teeth cleaned, while others can have drilling done on their teeth without anesthetic—vastly different levels of pain tolerance. It has absolutely nothing to do with spiritual understanding; it has to do solely with the nature of the organism.

What is absent in the sage is the secondary involvement in the pain, which is that quality of "What if this doesn't end? What will become of me? How will I survive it?" All of those questions relating to "What will *I* do if...." are gone. There still may be questions of "What will happen if...," but not questions of "What will *I* do?" It is this involvement that is the source of the suffering. The pain is in the moment. The suffering is the extension of the pain in the moment, no matter how intense, into the future.

Worry is a psychological projection into the future of what will become of me, which is not the planning of the moment. "Okay, I've got a problem here. How can I solve this problem? I have this pile of bills, and I don't have enough money to pay them all. How am I going to solve this problem?" The sage may well have to deal with that situation, and it may be enormously frustrating; however, what is absent is the suffering attendant to "What will become of me if I don't solve this?" The source of suffering is that involvement by the "me" in the unhappiness that is felt when one is in a bind, when there's no satisfactory way out.

Let's assume that for the last hour you haven't experienced suffering. Within that hour you probably weren't thinking, "Wow, this is great. I've had a whole hour without suffering." So it is with the sage. There isn't a sense of "Oh, how wonderful. I've got all this time without suffering." It's simply that the suffering doesn't arise—ever. So instead of just one hour, it never arises. So if you expand your experience of the absence of suffering for this last hour into a lifetime, you have the same experience as the sage—which is no experience.

♋ ♋ ♋

RENUNCIATION

What a dull and lifeless world it would be if in order to find God one had to give up life. Thankfully, the realization of our true nature can coexist with a passionate sexuality; it can coexist with a passionate love, and with all kinds of physical pleasures and sensory delights. I don't see that sex by its nature is an obstruction, or eating meat is an obstruction, or having lots of money is an obstruction. One can point to all of those things and say that you have to overcome them; that you like them too much, and it is your desire for these things that is inhibiting your realization of God. That's certainly one very popular notion with an accompanying methodology. The path of renunciation is a well-trodden path. But you would be hard pressed to find a direct causal link between renunciation and enlightenment. The spiritual path is littered with the corpses of renunciates who never achieved the enlightenment they were seeking. Mind you, they are lying right next to the tantric corpses that never achieved the enlightenment they were seeking through their method.

What I liked so much about encountering Ramesh was that he was a teacher who was very much of this world. He was a retired bank president, a family man, a husband, a father, a man who lived among us and interacted with us as a man, and yet there was this incredible understanding. That to me was the most attractive part of Ramesh and his teaching. He was living proof that it was not necessary to leave life in order to achieve the goal of God consciousness. What I learned through Ramesh was that the ultimate understanding was all-embracing: Consciousness was embracing everything so that everything was an expression of Consciousness; everything was an expression of God. To know God you touched life, you touched yourself—both sexually and metaphysically. You experienced the presence of God in everything. This teaching embraced everything, and that was awesome, truly awesome.

♋ ♋ ♋

DISTINCTIONS

As humans, we make distinctions between things. When a distinction is made to the effect that this is an arm, or that's a rug, the distinction is a product of the structure of the perceiving apparatus. The physicists are saying that in the most elemental sense the nature of something is dependent on that which is measuring. The body/mind apparatus determines the nature of the perception, and that which animates the apparatus is what we call Consciousness. Consciousness can be likened to electricity: When electricity flows through the dishwasher, it washes dishes; when it flows through the toaster, it makes toast—all because of the nature of the apparatus. It is the same electricity that is fueling these various outcomes, and it is the same Source that is fueling all of the human apparatuses *and* the non-human apparatus.

Humans are created with certain properties to perform various actions. So when the life force flows through them, they act in accordance with their nature. Take the example of a newborn child. The child has a nature totally independent from anything learned. From the moment you see a baby after it's birth you can already sense its nature. Each one has its own innate character, its own genetic predisposition.

Now, that predisposition is constantly modified by

life experiences, but the predisposition can also determine the life experiences. I have two children. My daughter, who is the eldest, was born one of the most blessed of human creatures. She had an incredibly beatific presence. She almost never fussed or cried. She was open, social, delighted with life, and people were drawn to this. She was like a magnet. Everybody wanted to hold her and cuddle her. So her world, her universe, was determined by this genetic predisposition with which she was born. As a result, the world appeared to her as a very friendly and welcoming place. Her basic open nature was reinforced by her environment.

My son was born as a much more normal child. His nature was such that he cried and fussed like most babies. You'd hand him to someone who would say, "Yeah, cute" and if he was crying, quickly hand him back. So from very early on his experience of the nature of the world was very different from hers. Not only was his basic nature different, but the world that he experienced was different as well.

So these combinations of factors, cumulative over time, dictated their respective natures: how they feel about themselves; how they interact with the world; the decisions they make. All of these are based on their nature. It is their nature that colors the "decision-making process." So when the life force flows through these two organisms, and they are faced with the same life situation, they will have very different reactions and make different decisions based on their nature. In each of their cases the ego says, "I made the decision." What is this "I" that made the decision? Was it not their basic genetic structure combined with all the subsequent conditioning?

How can anyone say realistically it was "my" decision? You didn't choose your genetic material. You didn't choose your DNA or the environment in which you were born. If you did, everyone would choose to be born a happy, joyous, loving, open creature so the world would love you, nurture you and support you. Who the hell would choose anything else?

With that understanding, you begin to have true humility for your blessings, and acceptance for your shortcomings and for the shortcomings of others. There begins to be an understanding and appreciation of the fact that a person who molests children did not choose to be such a monster. No one likes a child molester. There is no place on the planet where they are accepted and welcomed, loved, supported. Who would choose such a life? This does not mean that you approve of their acts and that you say, "Well, they're just part of life; let them teach school." That's not what I'm suggesting. With the understanding that every one is a product of the Source, it becomes impossible to hate. You can be disgusted, you can even lock the person up, you can castrate them, you can do all kinds of things to modify the socially unacceptable behavior, but whatever the response, it would be done without hatred.

FOURTEEN

The mind is its own place,
and in itself can make a Heav'n of Hell,
or a Hell of Heav'n.
John Milton (Paradise Lost)

PEACE

What most spiritual seekers are looking for at root is peace in life. Most people are not really looking for the peace of death. They're looking for peace while alive, peace when walking the earth, peace when interacting with others, peace when there's hardship, peace when things are not going their way, peace when people they love hurt them or die—peace amidst all of *that* is what most seekers want. This teaching points to the divine nature of everything that exists, no matter how hurtful or painful it might be. The understanding is that everything that exists is the manifestation of God. Normally, people don't have a problem with that idea as long as it refers to nice things: sunsets, puppies, the birth of a beautiful healthy child—all the wonders of creation. The problem comes with the ugly things, the despicable horror that is also part of life. It is in the acceptance of everything as the manifestation of God that the peace you are seeking comes. It is in the acceptance of *everything*.

Now, when I say acceptance, I do not mean that you have to approve of everything or that you treat everything equally. Acceptance is the understanding that all things have their root in the same Source, *including* all of your reactions, thoughts and feelings.

Trace your blessings back to their Source; trace the horrors in your life back to their Source and you will find the same Source. All too often, as we trace back the painful things in our life we stop here at the body/mind organism, and then guilt and blame are the result. When we trace our blessings back and we stop here at the body/mind organism, then pride is the result. But the deepest possible humility comes from knowing the Source from which spring both the blessings and the pain.

♋ ♋ ♋

THE END OF QUESTIONS

How would one recognize the thoughts that bubble up from the true Source versus what might be the ego bubbling up with an answer?

Well, I wouldn't make a distinction. The real question is, "What is the ego?" Is the ego somehow isolated from the Source?

Well, maybe not isolated, but not quite in touch, either.

In my model, you have the Source, which is the ground. What arises out of this Source may go through the ego, and when it goes through the ego, it is affected by the characteristics of that ego. You are describing the different ways that the Source reaches your conscious mind. In terms of this investigation, we are talking about taking that which reaches your conscious mind and tracing that back to its source. You may trace it back to this ego structure, but what is the source of the ego structure? What is its nature? Is it truly the originator of thoughts, or is the point of origination beneath it? Do you see?

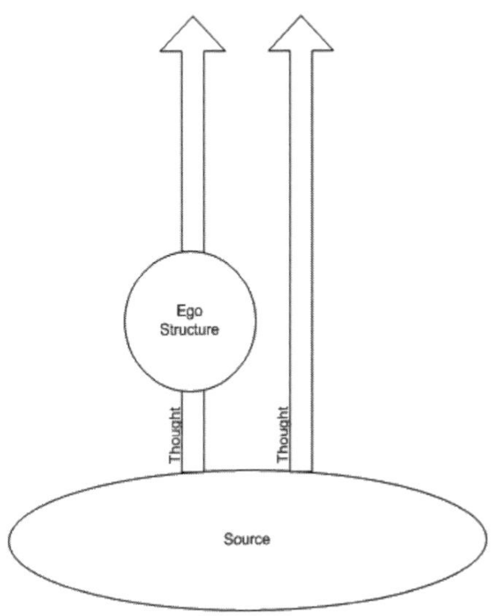

I think I do, but my question would still be how would one recognize when one is twisting or manipulating that which comes from the Source for one's own ego satisfaction?

What is this ego that is twisting things? You say, "I am twisting them. I am changing them." What is the nature of this "I" that is changing them? Is it independent of the Source?

So in the understanding, the notion that this ego is separate from the Source just disappears. It becomes irrelevant after that.

Yes, in the understanding that the ego is an *aspect* of the Source—that the Source functions through the ego—the ego stops being the enemy. It is seen as an aspect of the Source.

But that stuff doesn't arise in you any more, right? You don't sit around making distinctions between Source and ego any more unless, maybe, you're teaching. Do you?

Yes, in the final understanding, the question dissolves; the whole paradigm is no longer necessary. But for our purposes here, that paradigm is possibly useful as a teaching tool, as a way of pointing the attention so that a deeper understanding might occur.

Is the understanding that you talk about a process or something that can be indicated by some sort of final answer to the question?

Actually, the understanding that I talk about is the dissolution of the question, not the arrival at an answer.

So this Consciousness is like a field of potential. I know it's not a thing, because it can't be located, touched, or felt. It seems to me that Consciousness has a vibration potential or looks to be something, but it's still Consciousness, still that field of potential.

Right. The classic example is of the ocean and the wave: the ocean manifests into a form that we call a wave. The wave is never other than the ocean.

So it becomes an intuitive thought or an aspect of the ego. It's still the same thing. It hasn't changed what it is. Consciousness hasn't become something else.

Exactly. Consciousness is the ocean. The ocean can be foam, it can be spray, it can be waves, it can be in myriad forms, but regardless of the form, it is still ocean.

♋ ♋ ♋

LOOK AGAIN

If you look into the source of things in the way I have been suggesting, then you may well see that the claims of the ego are false and that the source of all thought, feeling and action is not the ego. That's something you have to find out for yourself. Under no circumstances can you rely on me for that. As you begin to see that the ego is a false claimer, the ego is disempowered. This period during which the ego is weakened but not gone is often experienced as a period of listlessness, disinterest, ennui. The liberation is in the deeper understanding that comes with the complete disempowerment of the ego, because then the identification shifts to our true nature, which is Consciousness. That is what we really are: Unlimited by the physical, unlimited by these forms but not separate from them.

♋ ♋ ♋

The Sage's mind is a mirror.
It grasps nothing. It regrets nothing.
It receives but does not keep.

Chuang Tzu

♋ ♋ ♋

THE PEACE THAT SURPASSES ALL UNDERSTANDING

There's a relative peace that comes and goes. I'm more interested in what St. Paul refers to as the "peace that surpasses all understanding." You've referred to it as an undercurrent that is here all the time, but we're not aware of it. For me there is inner turmoil, and to some degree, it's there most of the time. You remarked that I am not doing this to myself. It's all coming from the Source. I can see it's not from my parents or upbringing or my conditioning, so much as the immediate Source that sustains existence . . .

It is Source *functioning through* your upbringing, and your parents, and all the intermediate vehicles.

What is that Source? I don't know where to look for it. I can look within and I see what I feel and the thoughts that churn. I suspect it's not something in my personality. It's something beyond anything I could imagine or think.

This peace that surpasses all understanding *truly* surpasses all understanding.

Nothing to communicate.

So when you understand it, it's not the peace that surpasses all understanding any more.

Do you actually have a sense that there's fulfillment in the present moment? You don't lack anything?

Who are you talking to?

You.

And who is that? Wayne—Wayne Liquorman—this piece of meat with a mind attached to it? It has essentially the same qualities and characteristics as that piece of meat sitting over there; which is to say that sometimes it's hungry, sometimes it's thirsty, sometimes it's horny, sometimes it's happy, sometimes it's sleepy. It has the full range of needs, desires, frustrations, anger, happiness, and sadness—all those human qualities.

And they are different in perception than they were 20 or 30 years ago?

Yes, as it is in your case. You perceive things far differently than you did twenty years ago because there has been ongoing conditioning of the organism.

But isn't there some sort of shift in perspective after the enlightenment?

There is a shift in perspective, but this is where we have trouble with language. Perspective always presumes a point of perception. We usually think that when the perception shifts from one perspective to another, there's a shifting from one point to another. This final understanding is not a shift in perspective from a limited point to a universal point. The universal is not a point of perception. Therefore, the shift "in perspective" is not from a personalized, limited place to an impersonal, unlimited place. The shift is not to any "place" at all. So when you speak of "my perspective," we have to be clear to whom you are referring.

We often say that the sage's perspective is a perspective of the Total, because the limited perspective, in terms of an authoring "me," is no longer present; therefore, that veil is not covering the omnipresent Consciousness. So that *individual* veil is not present, but the perspective of the organism is still present, and that's what enables the sage to speak. If there were no personal perspective by the organism, the organism wouldn't be able to function, absolutely would not be able to function at all.

So, that's why I asked you to whom are you referring, of whom are you asking the question? Sages such as Nisargadatta Maharaj would answer those questions as if you were directly addressing Consciousness. The technique he used was to speak from the perspective of Consciousness. Now, the conclusion reached when listening to or reading the books or transcripts is that the body/mind mechanism named Maharaj had this perspective of Absolute Consciousness. But that is not completely accurate.

So the final understanding is literally unimaginable.

It is indeed! You can't imagine something that doesn't exist. So, this absence is what we're talking about. We can know the absence relative to the presence, but that absence when related to the presence becomes some *thing*, and that relative thing can be known. But when the nothing is unrelated, there is literally nothing to be known. Then it is the peace that surpasses understanding.

♋ ♋ ♋

WHAT IS SPIRITUAL?

To me all the tasks of life are by definition mundane, of-the-day, of-the-earth, and of-the-moment happenings. I make no particular distinction between sitting on a mountaintop in the Himalayas or working on the floor of the New York Stock Exchange.

My definition of what is spiritual has expanded to include everything—EVERYTHING—as an aspect of that One. If the person working at the stock exchange believes that "when I get these riches, then I will be fulfilled and I will be complete," he is no different from the fellow who is sitting on the mountaintop saying, "when I get this enlightenment then I will be fulfilled and complete." Both are seeking some *thing* to fulfill their own self. Both are equally ego-involved. A true sage can be working in the New York Stock Exchange, doing that task as part of his life work and his nature, without any more involvement than a true sage sitting on the top of a mountain answering the questions of the people who come to him.

Certain body/mind mechanisms are programmed to prefer quiet and solitude to activity and the presence of people. So the organism will seek that which it prefers. The acceptance or non-acceptance is much more fundamental than that. The acceptance underlies all that happens. The acceptance we talk about is not an experience; rather, it is an underlying animus, if you will. So we can talk about it as a thing, but it is not truly experiential as a thing. The acceptance is the absence of involvement, not the presence of dispassion.

COMPASSION

Compassion is a quality that is much valued and discussed in spiritual circles. But what is generally meant by this term "compassion?" The superficial meaning is "kindness:" a caring, heart-centered interaction in which the recipient is left with a good feeling. Compassion is actually deeper than that. I have seen what I would consider to be compassion from a sage, specifically Ramesh, which from the standpoint of the recipient was harsh. Ramesh isn't a harsh character, but sometimes the stripping away of a false belief, while compassionate, is not a gentle or sweet action.

As we get older, often we become encrusted with those beliefs that were used to create a sense of personal security. Of course, it never worked for very long. There is no security in life since the essence of life is change, so there's always that underlying tickle of uncertainty, of insecurity. The usual solution to this is to try and patch up the structure by applying new and stronger beliefs. Often the demolition of these encrusted false beliefs is a painful process; it leaves a person feeling uncomfortable, discontented and uncertain, but until these beliefs are removed, no further progress is possible.

♋ ♋ ♋

THE NOBILTY OF SEEKING

There is a presumption on the part of some seekers that what they are doing is noble and what everyone else is doing is essentially worthless. I don't happen to share that notion, but that is a very common perception among spiritual seekers: "I am searching for God! You're watching television. How can you possibility equate these two activities?" Well, I can very readily equate those two activities as being the activities that a particular body/mind organism has been programmed and conditioned to perform in a particular moment. The value we place on one or the other depends on whatever scale we're using, and the scale is essentially arbitrary.

If you go to your neighbor and say, "I'm on my way to a spiritual gathering. We're going to sit on the floor for an hour-and-a-half and talk about the nature of existence. It's not actually something you can know, but we're going to talk about it anyway for an hour-and-a-half, while our butts go numb. You want to come?" And he may well say, "Are you nuts? The big game is on TV in an hour." Most of the people in the world you literally could not force to attend an Advaita talk, and if you did, they would be miserable. So the recognition is that certain people are drawn to it, but most aren't.

Chogyam Trungpa wrote a book called *Cutting Through Spiritual Materialism.* When I read this book, which was relatively early on in my seeking, I was struck by the basic premise. He was saying that most seekers are seeking spiritual fulfillment in the same way that people seek financial fulfillment or sexual fulfillment or fulfillment from fame or fulfillment from material goods. He said that what was being sought was something material, and that people believed that when they got it, they would be better, happier, more complete. So there was essentially no difference between spiritual materialism and any other materialism. From where I sit today, I see that happening all the time.

♋ ♋ ♋

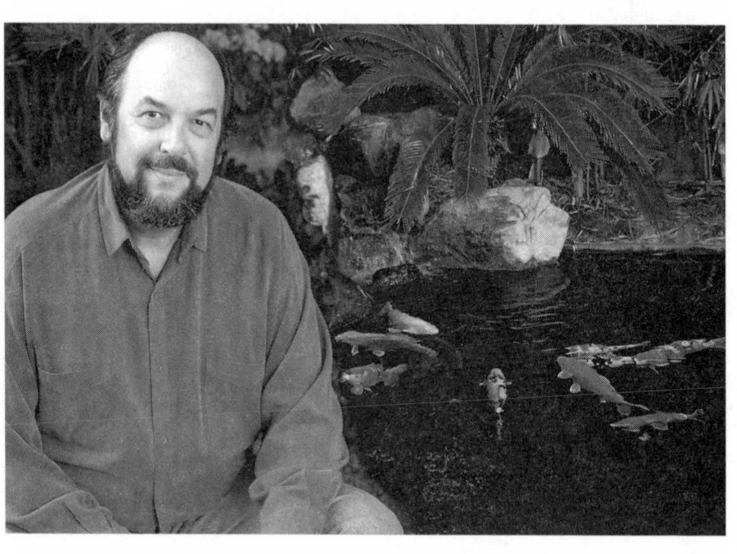

FIFTEEN

To be interested in the changing seasons
is a happier state of mind
than to be hopelessly in love with spring.
George Santayana

AMAZING GRACE

The pointer of this teaching is that what is functioning through the alcoholic, through the teetotaler, through the celibate, through the nymphomaniac, through *every* one and *every* action, is the same Source. It is *all* the functioning of the same Totality. Sometimes it is tragic, sometimes it's painful, sometimes there's tremendous suffering, sometimes there is enormous grace, and sometimes there's tremendous peace and freedom.

In my case, I was an alcoholic and this grace to stop drinking came. I was absolutely clear when it happened that it was not my doing, I didn't even want to stop drinking. My denial was so strong that I felt that I had my life together. Mind you, I was an absolute mess, but I would tell you that I was fine. In my case, that compulsion was removed in a heartbeat. The definition of grace that is so applicable here and that I like so much is grace as "unmerited favor from God"—*unmerited*. So it isn't that I finally purified myself or manufactured enough willpower to make it go away. It was *unmerited* favor in the instant that occurred. And I was given this doorway out of addiction and the energy to walk through it in that moment. That was 1985. It is not that I, through some power that I exert, don't drink; it is that the compulsion to drink simply doesn't happen anymore and thus I was "saved" from a miserable alcoholic life and death. I call that grace.

♋ ♋ ♋

EFFORTS

Acceptance is not something that we can generate. The acceptance, when it comes, is very much like grace because it makes the most intolerable situations tolerable. And whether it's poverty or cancer, or some other condition that is having an undesirable effect on one's life, the acceptance that this is present in the moment does bring peace. It doesn't mean that you have to like it, nor is acceptance a suggestion that you stop making efforts to bring about a change. Efforts may well arise, and the next effort may provide the desired result. We can only do what we do and then see what happens next. The pointer of the Teaching is that both the doing and the result will be part of the same functioning, with you as the instrument through which that functioning happens.

So, acceptance does not remove the immediate problem, it does not make the circumstances of your life change in accordance with how you want them to be. It removes the suffering attendant to the problem, and that is what we call peace . . . the peace that surpasses all understanding.

♋ ♋ ♋

THE SAGE ORGANISM

The sage is the human organism through which the event we call enlightenment has happened. What characterizes the sage-organism in the wake of this event is the *absence* of something, not the presence of something. Most people think the sage *gets* enlightenment, but the organism we call the sage has something *less,* rather than something more. The sage is what everyone and everything truly is: that Consciousness which is *always* present. It is present when the human organism is in deep sleep; it is present when the organism is in the waking state. It is omnipresent. And the sage does not believe himself to be otherwise. It is not that he believes himself to be That, it is that he does not believe himself to be separate. What the seekers mind always supplies is a "me" that knows this Truth, but in the sage there is no "me" at all.

That's why in terms of spiritual materialism this teaching has no payoff. In this teaching, enlightenment is defined as the *dissolution of the seeker,* not the attainment by the seeker of that which he's seeking. Most religions and many spiritual movements hold on to their customers by promising them a huge end benefit, saying, "You're going to get *sat-chit-ananda;* you're going to get infinite bliss; you're going to get infinite peace; you're going to get infinite unity and oneness." This Advaita teaching points to the fact that, yes, the infinite peace will be there, but YOU won't be there. IT will be there. Thus, it is no surprise that this kind of pure Advaita has such a limited appeal.

The Teaching demands nothing less than the death of the ego. And the ego will not kill itself. It will pay lip service to the notion that oblivion is what it wants, but when it gets right to the edge, it cannot take that last step.

It's like the story of the man who falls over a cliff and half way down he grabs onto a branch. He's hanging there dangling over an abyss:

He yells up, "Help me! Can somebody help me?"

A voice calls down, "I'll help you."

"Oh, thank goodness somebody's up there. You'll help me?"

"Yes, I am God. I am here and I will help you."

"Wow! What a relief! Okay, God, what do you want me to do?"

God says, "Let go."

And the man yells, "Is there anybody else up there?"

The ego is not capable of doing anything and that includes killing itself.

♋ ♋ ♋

WHO AM I?

I've been asking Ramana's question, "Who am I?" for a long time now, and I can't find an answer.

Well, I'm not sure that there is a True answer.

Well, that's good to know. That means I can stop looking.

No, not at all. It does not negate the value of the inquiry. The inquiry has an effect quite apart from providing you with a True conceptual answer.

The only answer I can come up with is Awareness.

Okay, we'll give that answer a 5.6 from the panel of judges.

It's the only thing I can't eliminate.

The point of the inquiry really is much deeper than that. When you have an answer to who I am or what I am, it is an interim answer. It may have usefulness in the moment, but eventually it needs to be scrutinized. Whatever your answer is, somebody else can argue it with you. You may well end up doubting it yourself. So, how do you figure out whether that's the right answer?

How do you?

The ultimate pointer is that every answer that is conceptual is limited. Every answer that you can articulate and know is, by its very nature, limited and at some point must be called into question or doubted.

So my suspicion that there is no answer is maybe closer.

Actually, I would say that there are a vast number of answers.

I understand that what we're really speaking of is beyond the mind and beyond concepts. That I get.

Okay, but when you get that, that's conceptual also.

I know. You just keep going around in circles.

You do. So, never mind.

♋ ♋ ♋

THIS PERFECT MOMENT

As one's understanding deepens, it is understood that that which is material is spiritual, that includes everything that exists, not just the sunsets, the puppies, and the rainbows and dolphins, but also the sadists, the rapists, the murderers. *Everything* is spiritual.

Of course, we don't invite psychopathic murderers into our homes. We don't entrust our valuables to known theives. We still have practical considerations, but there is the understanding that even the foulest creatures are *aspects* of the Source. The same manifest energy that creates saints, creates sinners. All are aspects of the same thing, and that which they are aspects of, is spiritual. This becomes the reality. That's the beauty of this teaching: *anything* that you do is a happening, part of the natural flow of What Is.

It is such an incredible relief. It is such an enormous freedom. The load lightens as the understanding deepens that every quality you have—good or bad—is an aspect of Source.

As you are in this moment—in this very instant—is *Perfect* and could not be otherwise.

A CHAT

Where are you from?

I am from Pennsylvania.

Ramesh did a couple of retreats in Pennsylvania years ago up in Bangor—Delaware Water Gap area.

Wow! Is he coming here again?

No, he no longer travels. Have you read his books?

No, I just heard about him from a friend. Ramesh is fully enlightened.

As opposed to partially enlightened?

I think you get there slowly—except for Ramana Maharshi.

Enlightenment is like death. You get there slowly, but it is always sudden when it happens. So it is like asking are you fully dead.

It is different from death. I think you are either alive or dead.

Exactly.

Are you saying enlightenment is exactly like death?

In the either/or of it, yes.

That does not sound too appealing to me.

That is why Ramesh has relatively few disciples.

So how does this happen?

Grace.

By praying?

Is praying Grace?

You pray for grace. Does it take away all confusion in life, and pain and sorrow?

No.

What is enlightenment then? Looks like you know what it is.

Enlightenment is the end of personal involvement in the pain and sorrow and, thus, the end of suffering. The pain and sorrow continue as part of life.

You mean Ramesh feels upset, depressed, etcetera?

Pain, sadness, etcetera. I was with him when his son died. He was quite grief-stricken, but there was no "me" to be involved in the grief and thus suffer. There was simply deep and profound grief.

What is the "me?" Isn't it the grief itself? How are you separating the two?

It is a notional separation, a way of pointing.

So if someone says unkind things to Ramesh, he gets upset too?

He has preferences, likes and dislikes, just like any human.

Does he have more faith in God than us?

He has something LESS. Not something more.

The less is the no "me" to be involved in the grief?

Exactly.

Does Ramesh worry about the future, whether he will have money, and all that?

Worry, no; plan, yes.

I assume he is peaceful like Ramana Maharshi?

Do you think Ramana was peaceful every moment, or rather, that he exhibited peaceful behavior every moment?

I am sure he was at peace.

So am I. But he could be at peace and still display anger or frustration.

Are you saying there cannot be worry when there is peace? These distinctions are too subtle.

Worry is usually about what will happen to "me."

How can someone not worry about that?

If there is no "me," there is no "me" to worry about.

But there is family, your health; all of these are the "me." So the sign of enlightenment is the absence of worry in the person?

No, it is the absence of the "me." There are no signs.

I will take the absence of worry for now, but if I get the absence of the "me," I will take that too.

But the worry comes with the one who would take it. YOU are the "me" that can't get its absence.

So there is no way out of this?

Exactly.

Then is there something called enlightenment or is that just an illusion?

It is what we call the event when the illusion of the "me" disappears—or more precisely, DIES.

This is quite clear except for the how to get it.

WHO would get it?

But these discussions will always go in circles, because we always talk with reference to a "me" who gets it. Without talking about the "me," how can we talk about it?

Yes, as long as you think about a "me" getting it, you are screwed.

So nobody gets it because the one that gets it is the problem. But then it happens, so to whom does it happen?

Not *to* someone, *through* someone.

And how does that someone know?

How do you know that you just said that?

I just know.

Exactly.

But lots of people believe it has happened to them, and I am not so sure they are right.

Definitely, believing it does not make it so. But if it is so, it requires no belief.

Are you enlightened?

That event happened THROUGH me.

Are you like Ramesh?

I am much taller.

So you never worry about the "me?"

No ME to worry about.

So here is what I really want to ask. If you are unemployed, will you not worry about the future at all and just trust God?

Worry, no; project what will happen if I don't get a job and then go out and make some sort of effort to find work, yes...but only because it is my nature to do so. Someone else might sit on their ass and wait for something to appear.

That is very clear. Of course, trying not to worry doesn't work; it just has to happen, I guess. So perhaps it is all grace, as you said. Still seems unfair why some don't worry and others do. But I suppose there is nothing one can do about it.

You will have to complain about the unfairness to the proper authorities, though it might be agreed that you already have an unfair amount of the world's bounty.

I asked for that, I guess.

And if you get the fairness you seek, you are going to lose a lot.

I get what you are saying. Thanks again. You have been very helpful.

You are most welcome. I am glad you found it helpful.

♋ ♋ ♋

INDEX

A

B

C

D

E

F

G

T

As of this writing (September 2004) Wayne Liquorman is traveling the world, sharing his Teaching in talks, seminars and retreats. If you have found the contents of this book to be of interest and would like to meet Wayne, details of his schedule can be found on the Advaita Fellowship website:

www.advaita.org

Or you may write or phone:

The Advaita Fellowship
P.O. Box 3479
Redondo Beach, CA 90277
USA

Tel. 310-376-9636

More From Advaita Press

A Duet of One by Ramesh S. Balsekar

Here Ramesh uses the Ashtavakra Gita as a vehicle for an illuminating look at the nature of duality and dualism.
Softcover 224 Pages $16.00

Who Cares?! by Ramesh S. Balsekar

This is the boook we recommend to those asking for a book that will describe the essence of Ramesh's teaching. Ramesh's ability to cut through to the simple heart of complex ideas is a joy to experience.
Softcover 220 Pages $16.00

Acceptance of What IS by Wayne Liquorman

A look at Advaita through the eyes of the most unlikely of Sages. Wayne's expression of his spiritual understanding is at once irreverent and profound. We laugh, sometimes joyously, sometimes uncomfortably but always with the recognition that we are in the presence of a Master. Softcover 304 Pages $16.00

Your Head In The Tiger's Mouth by Ramesh S. Balsekar

A superb overview of the Teaching. Transcribed portions of talks Ramesh gave in his home in Bombay during 1996 and 1997.
Softcover 472 Pages $24.00

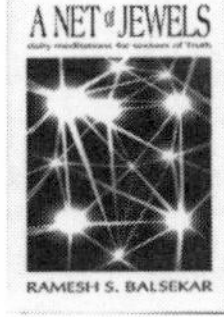

A Net Of Jewels by Ramesh S. Balsekar

A handsome gift volume of jewels of Advaita, selections from Ramesh's writings presented in the format of twice daily meditations.
Hardcover 384 Pages $25.00

Consciousness Speaks by Ramesh S. Balsekar

Ramesh's most accessible and easy to understand book. Recommended both for the newcomer to Advaita and the more knowledgeable student of the subject.
Softcover 392 Pages $19.00

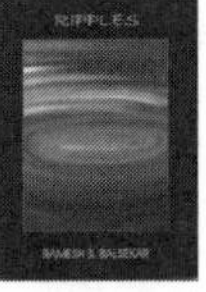

Ripples by Ramesh S. Balsekar

A brief and concise introduction to Ramesh's Teaching. Perfect to give to friends. Softcover 44 Pages $6.00

SEE NEXT PAGE FOR ORDERING DETAILS

www.advaita.org

NO WAY *for the spiritually advanced* by Ram Tzu

No Way is a unique blending of wit, satire and profound spiritual insight. One minute we are howling with unconstrained laughter, the next we are squirming in self-conscious recognition as Ram Tzu holds up a perfect mirror and then gleefully points out that we aren't wearing any clothes.
Softcover - 112 Pages $13.00
Also available on Audio Cassette $15.00

==============

If unavailable at your bookstore, these titles and many others may be ordered directly from the Advaita Press Store at **www.advaita.org**

OR

Send check, money order or Visa/Mastercard or American Express number (include expiration date and billing zip code) for the indicated amount plus shipping as noted below to:

Advaita Press
P.O. Box 3479 NM1
Redondo Beach, CA 90277
USA

Shipping & Handling:

In U.S. :

Surface mail: First book $4.00. Add $1.00 each additional.
Airmail: First book $6.00. Add $1.00 each additional book.

Outside U.S.Å.:

Canada Airmail: First Book $8.00. Add $4.00 each additional.
International Airmail: $12.00 per book.
International Surface mail: $6.00 per book

Payment in U.S. dollars via credit card, check or money order payable on a U.S. bank. No Eurochecks please.

www.advaita.org